BREAK FREE

One man's journey to end the suffering cycle of abuse

By L Goodrick

Contents

Introduction

One evening, I was sat talking to a friend and, out of nowhere, she told me that she had been sexually abused as a child. Now, 40 years later, it still affects her. I could see the pain and hurt in her eyes as they gradually filled with tears. She had never dealt with the pain, anger or the shame that us survivors put on ourselves. Rather than looking for help, she went down the same path of self-harm and despair that many of us do

Unknown to her, my own trauma started at age 5 with sexual abuse, which lasted for 11 years. I also lived through mental and emotional abuse that involved me, my sister and mother for 30 years. And I made 2 serious attempts at suicide, addictions to food, illegal drugs and medications, plus alcohol abuse and even becoming homeless and, on top of that, I overcame a diagnosis that normally limits people's lives.

I'm not just a survivor. I've broken free without help from others and I'm living a life I never thought would be possible.

If you've identified with any of the above then this book could be the one you've been searching for to break free. When you read how I've made it through, you'll know that you can too.

I share the story of my darkest times and the most painful truths with love and honesty in a hope that you know, no matter what you've been through or who has hurt you, you too can break free from pain and suffering.

I have 3 questions:

1. How amazing and free will you feel after realising your own truths?

2. Are you ready to break free and become the person that you've always wanted to become?

3. How many new connections and opportunities will you make once you take your power back and live proudly?

This book is not just my story, it's about yours too. At the end of each chapter, I will take you through the skills that have worked for me and they are all backed by science but don't worry I won't bore you with hundreds of pages of theories on several types of therapies that only work for some but not all.

The skills in *Break Free* will develop your courage and strengths. Then in chapter 10, we will work together to develop your clarity to get the most from the skills you've learnt. You will become the person you've always wanted to be, no matter what challenges you face. The skills you learn will grow with you.

There's no point in constantly thinking *why did they hurt you?* or *why choose me?* All that does is keep us in 'victim mode'. No one will ever be able to give you a reason, so stop waiting for someone to save you and save yourself.

Life is 10% what's happened to you and 90% how you react to it.

It doesn't matter how much you hope and wish that your life would change; nothing will happen without you putting the skills to work. But you're not alone in your journey: I am right here with you and you can reach out to me at any point through the links at the end of chapter 10.

I have tried to recreate events, locals, and convocations from my memories of them. To maintain their animosities in some instances I have changed their names of individuals and places, I have changed some identifying characteristics and details such as physical properties, occupations, and places of residence.

My Promise and Commitment

I can't promise that this book will change how others treat you. But I know that once you discover who you truly are, through the 'who am I?' skill, you will be strong enough to not let them mistreat you ever again and your future possibilities will be endless.

I don't have a PhD, nor am I a therapist. I am just an average guy that's lived in and through pain. From my own experiences with therapists and over years of research, I have moulded techniques to help with trauma and created my own methods that have worked for me and others. Now is the time to start living the life you deserve!

Just because life hasn't always been the easiest or the kindest doesn't mean the things that have happened to you will decide your future. It all starts with you saving yourself!

Sending you love and light until you find your own.

Lee Goodrick

2020

You are loved.

Chapter 1

The Start of it All.

'The start of my darkness'

One of the earliest memories I have is of sharing a bath with my dad when I was around 5 years old. This wasn't abnormal for our family to do. Even though we received free coal and always had plenty of hot water, my parents grew up in the era of air raid shelters and food rationing and I guess you could call it a tradition.

This was the first time I recall my dad encouraging me to touch his penis. At the time, I didn't think this was wrong; I was only 5 and this kind of incident happened often. I normally shared a bath with my sister, Grace, which wouldn't normally cause a problem as most siblings are around the same age. But there are 14 years between us so, as you can imagine, at times it could be quite awkward especially as I got older and started to ask questions about our differences.

Grace had to put up with a lot from her little brother. Of course, we got up to the same antics as any other family. One incident sticks in both our memories: me sneaking into her room while she was out and sticking my fingers down all of her lipstick tubes. It was the 80s, so you can imagine all the amazing sticks full of colour would attract a child. Still, it must have been highly annoying!

One afternoon, I was off school as it was a teachers' training day and Mum had taken me into town with her so that she could go shopping. I'm sure I was a hindrance but I loved 'our' time. While we were out I needed the toilet and, at that age, I had to go into the ladies with Mum so that she could take me into a cubical. I remember my feet swinging under the toilet bowl and, as Mum bent down to help me to pull my pants up, she stepped back and stared at me. I thought I was in trouble for something. I quickly pulled up my pants and we washed our hands and got a taxi home.

Once home, Mum dumped the shopping bags and hurried me upstairs into the bathroom. She stripped me off to give me a flannel wash and I vividly remember seeing her dunking my pants into the basin and scrubbing at them. The water turned a murky red and, without any explanation, Mum knelt to me and said, "don't tell your father," as if I had done something wrong and I was being told off.

God only knows what she thought I'd been doing but we never spoke about it again and I never told anyone for the rest of my life – until now.

Just like all kids, I was naughty at times and I would mess around to get something that I wanted. One of these things was to sleep in Mum's bed with her, which meant that my dad would be cast out to sleep in my single bed in the next room. The times that I won meant that Dad couldn't come into my bed for 'cuddles' in the middle of the night. It wasn't ever just for a cuddle; he would wait until everyone was asleep then sneak into my bed to molest me.

I would get a visit a couple of times a week. He would sneak into my room, climb into bed with me and then he would wrap his arms around me so tight that I would be completely restricted, unable to move an inch. He would always put a hand over my mouth so I could only breathe through my nose. I would often disassociate with my surroundings and with the terrifying situation he was putting me in. It was like having an out of body experience. I would blank everything out to the point where I couldn't hear him grunting into the back of my head as he abused me. I guess it was my brain protecting me from what was going on.

Even though I managed to block out what was happening, I can still remember the smell of his hands and their rough texture against my face. These visits would continue for the next 4 years or so.

By age 11, my weight had ballooned to 12 stone and I had discovered I could easily disconnect from my emotions by eating. I could blur out anything that caused me upset or distress. It was amazing but my weight was beginning to have an impact on my life. Not only did I struggle to take part in activities at school but I had also started to get bullied because of it. This was the start of a very vicious cycle that would stick with me for most of my life: the more I suffered from my environment the more I would eat to compensate for the pain that I felt.

In an attempt to help me lose some of the weight that I was gaining, Mum had started to send me to school with a packed lunch in the hope she could help me to have some control over my rapidly expanding waistline. But, back when I was at school, there wasn't the information available on diet and nutrition like there is today and one of Mum's friends had lost weight using a liquid meal replacement shake but Unfortunately, it just gave the bullies even more fuel they already had and they branded the shakes as 'fat fast'.

The only way I could escape the bullying was to pay them off with the money Dad had given me for the tuck shop. It was a terrible situation to be in but I was moving up to secondary school soon so I hoped everything would change for the better.

But things were about to get a whole lot more complicated.

Mum had me later in life – she was 42. My dad had wanted a child of his own (my siblings were from my mum's first marriage). Babies born to older mothers are often at a higher risk of developing complications, such as learning difficulties and chromosomal abnormalities. Mum was advised to have tests to see if I was at risk of developing any of these and I tested positive for Klinefelter syndrome. This affects around 1 in every 660 males and is where boys are born with an extra X chromosome, giving them XXY instead of XY. This causes problems with normal puberty development and affects the growth of body hair, development of muscle mass and bone density. Those with the condition are at higher risk of undeveloped left-brain functions, which includes difficulties with spoken and written language. Those with Klinefelter syndrome, or KS for short, can have issues with gaining weight easily and have undeveloped testes, meaning that our testicles are often 6 times smaller than the average man's. Plus, we can't start puberty without testosterone medication which in itself can cause many unwanted side effects, especially increased aggression.

The only bonus was that I got out of school for half a day to go to the doctors for my weekly injections. My parents had decided not to tell me or anyone else that I had the condition. Maybe if they had, adults around me would have been a little more forgiving of my mood swings and outbursts of aggression. The testosterone injections worked great at giving my body the hormone it was missing and allowed me to start puberty around the same time as everyone else at my new school.

A few months into treatment, I was experiencing huge peaks and drops in my hormone levels and my mood was all over the place. It was making me incredibly angry most of the time and, combined with the trauma of my abuse, I was pretty much out of control.

***

It was the start of the six-week-long summer holiday, which is a huge amount of time when you're a kid. There wasn't much to do, so Dad started to take me over to one of his friend's houses. I guess he thought it would give Mum a break from me constantly being around. I was 13 and Dad's friend, Alex, used to fix old cars, which would have seemed a great pastime for any teenage kid. But I would have been far happier sat in front of the TV all day. I didn't have many friends, which made me quite lonely. Mum used to encourage me to get out and get some fresh air.

Alex lived in the middle of nowhere. His house was surrounded by fields and horses roamed freely. I loved to feed and pet them whenever I could get close enough. Mum hated Alex, he gave her the creeps, so he was banned from visiting our house. Mum loved our house to be clean and tidy and Alex was always in dirty overalls. He smelt of sweaty socks and car oil. He was always tinkering with an old rusty car or a motorbike that he had acquired from some scrap dealer and was trying to do them up to resell them cheaply. He just wasn't Mum's cup of tea.

After a while, once I had got used to being around Alex, Dad had started to leave me there while he went to visit his sister. She lived a few miles away and I remember thinking that I must be a real pain in the ass as no one wants to spend any time with me.

As much I liked being in the fields, I didn't get on with Alex. He would always try and force me to wrestle with him as soon as we were alone.

He would grab hold of the back of my neck and try and force me to the ground. He'd say, "Come on, you're a big lad. You can do better than that." Followed quickly by, "Don't start crying or I'll give you something to cry about." Every now and again, he would force me onto my back and straddle my head between his knees, forcing my face into his crotch. The experience would make me physically sick. I was overridden with fear; I felt powerless and I just wanted my Mum.

Dad would take me to Alex whenever I got too much for Mum to cope with. One August afternoon, we went over again, this time it was going to be for the whole day. Dad had arranged for Alex to watch me for the day while he went to see his sister and some of his old friends. I only discovered this when we were 5 minutes away. Alex lived about an hour's drive from home so there was no way I could have walked back.

Before I could think clearly and make up an excuse, we had arrived and Dad dropped me off at the top of the path. Alex shouted up to me, "Oi! Come down here. I wanna show you summat." Immediately, I felt dread that I was in for another wrestling match but, as I started to walk down the path and in between the never-ending sea of old rusty cars, I could see what he was stood next to. It was covered in a huge blue plastic sheet and as I moved closer, I could see he was stood with another man that I'd never seen before. As I approached the car, Alex said, "This is my mate, Phil. He used to hang about with me and ya dad."

Phil said, "Alright, cocker. How you doin'?"

"I'm okay, thank you," I replied and stepped back a little from them both. I just didn't have a good feeling about him.

I started to walk away when Alex said, "Oi! Don't bugger off. We need your help with lifting summat out of the car pit."

As soon as he said that I could felt like all the blood in my body drain into my feet. I hated small confined places but Alex assured me it would only take a minute and then I could go and see the horses.

Alex had his arm around my shoulder and told me I had nothing to worry about. As we walked over to the entrance of the car pit, he told me to go down first as there wasn't much room. He grabbed the back of my neck and said he didn't want me to fall. I started to panic as I got to the bottom of the closed-in hole.

I turned around and Alex was behind me and Phil was at the top of the steps, pulling the cover over. I started to panic again and I began to think of the times Dad had trapped me in bed. I was now crying and shouting at the top of my voice to be let out. The next thing I remember was my face being held against the wall as someone was raping me. All I could think about was the pain. It completely took over everything and then I must have blacked out.

The next thing I knew was light flooding into the bottom of the pit. Alex yelled at me to get up. "You're filthy. I need to sort you out before the Mrs gets back."

I felt nothing: no pain, no fear. I had a ringing in my ears and when I stood up I felt wet and cold. I pulled up my shorts and started to walk back up to the top of the entrance. I couldn't see Phil; he'd gone. The light was blinding and it took me a while to see clearly again. I followed Alex into the house and he told me that I had pissed myself and he needed to wash my clothes before his Mrs got home from work. He took me into the shower and stripped me and told me to get washed while he put my clothes into the washer.

I was dazed and still didn't know what had just happened. I got in the shower and I remember looking down at my feet. Blood trickled down my leg. I felt sick and my ears were still ringing. I washed and got out to dry. The shower room was small, with a stone floor. It was freezing. When I opened the door, my clothes were on the floor. I guessed they had been washed but they were still wet. But I put them back on anyway.

Alex's wife had arrived home and I could hear her from the hallway where I was stood. Alex shouted for me to come into the lounge. He had told her we were wrestling again and that I'd fallen into the car pit (there is no way anyone would have believed that: there was a car covering the hole for a start!). She looked at me like I was an inconvenience. She said there were some apples in the kitchen and why don't I go and feed the horses before it gets dark. As I was grabbing the apples, I could hear both of them shouting at each other. I didn't care what it was about; I just wanted Mum.

It must have been early evening as Dad had just arrived back and Alex had come out to see us off. "We had a great time wrestling but I think I took it a bit far this time. I tripped him up and he smacked his face on the wall. Probably best not to talk about it, aye, Lee?"

I got into the car and started to cry. It was a mixture of pain from sitting down and maybe relief that it was over. But I couldn't feel relaxed because now I was in another closed space with my dad. He put his hand on my knee and asked if I was okay. At that point, I wished I was brave enough to have opened the car door and jumped. But instead, I just said yes, stopped crying and stared out of the window for the whole journey home. Dad never took me back to see Alex after that and I never spoke of it.

A few weeks later, Dad had organised an ice-skating party at our local rink for my 14th birthday. People thought I was spoilt; I guess I was, in a way, but not for the right reasons. I was looking forward to the party and had invited some school friends. It was rare for me as I didn't make friends easily. My KS created issues with communication and I felt so disconnected from the world that I wasn't able to form real connections. On the day of the party, we had all arrived at the rink and were stood at the desk getting our skates. Dad was stood next to the desk talking to one of the assistants and I overheard Dad telling her that my Uncle Alex had paid for the lot as a birthday gift. Instantly, I felt sick. I wanted the floor to swallow me up. I wanted to tell everyone to fuck off. Instead, I put on a happy face and pretended I was my normal self.

You're probably thinking *why didn't I tell anyone what had happened?*

When you've suffered years of abuse, you just think it's normal and it must be happening to everyone else and that no one talks about it. You don't think like an adult at 15 years old or at least I didn't. And back in the 90s it wasn't spoken about on TV or in schools. Even if I had told someone, who would believe me? Mum knew and we didn't speak about it. My dad was a mean bastard and he would taunt my Mum and Grace, making their lives hell. The last thing I was going to do was to add fuel to an already burning fire.

Grace was from my Mum's first marriage. Maybe that's why Dad bullied her so much. I'll never know for sure and, years later, when I spoke to Grace about our childhood she also had no clue. My sister was an incredible support for Mum in every way possible. She used to take me everywhere with her, mostly to get me from underneath Mum's feet. Even years later, when Grace had left home to get married, she would still see Mum most days.

I will always be grateful to Grace. It couldn't have been easy to keep returning to a house where she had spent her teenage years being threatened and emotionally abused by my dad.

The sexual abuse had stopped by the time I reached 15 years old, It had gone on for 10 years and maybe my eating habits had paid off; he no longer wanted to touch me. Thanks to the hormones, by 16, I had started to grow hairs in places other guys had at 13. By now, I was hitting 18 stone. Mum would describe me as "built like a brick shit house" and that "Lee lives to eat, rather than eats to live!"

Looking back on it, I now think it's a little cruel but growing up I didn't think much of it. It was just how it was and Mum would not have intentionally hurt me. I guess it was a way of making light-hearted fun of my weight.

***

At 15, I signed up to do an apprenticeship in hairdressing. It would consist of 4 days a week in a local salon and a day a week at college. It was something positive in my life and, for a change, I didn't need to rely on my dad for anything. It took me a couple of years to get my qualification but, once I had it, I could apply to big chain salons to become a technician, which involved me going to Manchester for 6 weeks to do my advanced training. It was the first time I had been away from home and I absolutely thrived. The only downsides were the inescapable mirrors and always being surrounded by fashion-conscious people. In the 9 years I had been working, my weight had ballooned again. At the age of 25, my weight was at an all-time high of 23 stone. I was huge!

Home life was getting progressively worse and my dad was at a whole new level. He was more volatile than he had ever been and was now becoming aggressive towards Mum, not just mentally but now he had started pushing her around and threatening her. Honestly, I don't know how she used to cope. She had rheumatoid arthritis, which gave her a great deal of pain especially in her hands. But she never moaned about anything. It probably had something to do with her stubbornness; no matter how much mental abuse or physical pain she was in, you'd never be able to tell.

The pressure must have been unbearable at times, but she never faulted in being a great Mum. The house was always spotless, we had a constant supply of freshly washed and pressed clothes and, for as long as I can remember, we would have a home-cooked roast at the end of every day, even though she worked full-time at the local hospital.

She was a brilliant mum. I just wish I'd known her as a woman and not just as my mum.

Chapter 2

Breaking the Mould.

'Happiness doesn't just happen you have to go after it'

Something had to be done. My weight was spiralling out of control and the worse I felt, the more I ate! Even though I knew deep down it wouldn't make me feel any better, it still gave me comfort. If my environment or routine changed, making me feel unsure or scared, food would quickly make me feel a whole lot better and my treats were always there for me, no matter what.

In hairdressing, I learnt how to hide my emotions and put up a front, showing whatever face was needed for the client. On the back of the door in the staffroom was a sign that read 'stage door'. At first, I massively struggled with this but, after a while, I was an expert at becoming whoever my clients needed me to be.

In all honesty, that was far less stressful than trying to wade through all my mixed emotions. Love wasn't a word or feeling I was used to. My parents never told me that they loved me; I was just meant to know. Mum showed it by taking care of me and always giving me a beautiful home to live in. I never went without and I was always well fed. As for my dad, somewhere deep down I knew he was a good person – he just had his own demons that he didn't know how to deal with so he took it out on his family.

Maybe he had been abused in that way when he was a kid and he was just repeating that behaviour. It 100% did not make it okay, nor did it mean I could understand why he didn't break the pattern of abuse. It would be a mystery to me for the rest of my life. Most people would ask their grandparents to fill in the blanks about their parents' lives. But both sets of my grandparents had died either before I was born or within my first few years.

I travelled a hell of a lot with hairdressing, which meant I was alone most of the time. I had developed a fear of dominant men with deep voices, especially the ones that were confrontational. In later years, I would learn that these were my 'triggers' – something that would bring back flashbacks or feelings from my past. It wouldn't matter where I was or what I was doing, a trigger could happen at any time: on a train station platform or even a guy at work that I knew well. If he shouted to another person over the sound of a hairdryer, I could just start crying.

To anyone else it would look ridiculous, as if I was crying for no reason. I got great at thinking on my feet; I was able to make something up on the spot!

I relied on the one thing that wouldn't judge me, food. But I had to do something to get this weight off. It wasn't doing anything positive for me. I'd never been on a real diet and I had never done any form of exercise so I had no idea where to start.

Until one Sunday afternoon when I was at home watching the London Marathon on TV (no doubt stuffing my face). I became mesmerised by the elite woman runners. They made running at speed look so effortless and, out of nowhere, I had the idea that I was going to become an elite distance runner!

It didn't even enter my mind that they had been running since they could walk or even that I had a weight issue; I had made my mind up.

I had found the solution, now I just needed to find the method to get me there. I didn't know anyone that was into fitness so I had nobody to ask. Besides, I didn't want anyone to know my plan for fear of being made to look like a fool. So, one day after work, I went into the city to one of the huge bookshops to where I felt totally out of my depth. After an hour of searching, I had found all the sports autobiographies but they weren't going to be of any use. I needed the technical knowhow. One of the books I came across was *The Lore of Running* by Tim Noakes MD. It looked impressive and was super-heavy so I thought this guy must know what he's talking about. When I got home, I read the whole book in 2 days straight. It was now time to get out and do my first ever run.

WOW!

Looking back, I have to laugh. It wasn't a run or a jog – more of an extremely slow shuffle. I don't even think I lifted my feet off the ground. It was that bad. I think I only managed to do 15 minutes before I could feel my heart beating like a drum behind my eyes. I had the stark realisation this was going to be a hell of a lot harder than I first imagined!

I went back to my book for guidance and read about running shoes. They seemed nothing like my old, battered gym pumps from school. I was going to need some proper running shoes so, after I had been paid, I went to a sports shop to see what I could find. Just walking in was incredibly intimidating. I didn't have any confidence outside of a salon and I cared very much what others thought about me. Eventually, I found a section at the back that was labelled 'running' and I found a pair that seemed suitable and were within my budget.

My next task was my diet. I went back to the bookshop but it proved to be a lot harder to pick something out that would be suitable. I needed enough calories to recover but also to help me lose the fat. There were hundreds of diet books on the shelves. *The Lore of Running* kept talking about 'nutrition' rather than one particular diet so I had a wander and took myself off to the academic section of the shop and found *Sports Nutrition* by Nancy Clarke, which looked simple to understand but advanced in the areas I needed. Just like before, I studied that book until I knew it almost word for word!

I had adopted Mum's stubbornness, which was a useful trait to have. If I was going to get to my goal, I was going to have to see it with blinkers on and not allow myself to get distracted. Over the next few months, one shuffle at a time, I realised I was more than shuffling – my shuffle had turned into a jog without me even knowing. I was absolutely loving my new-found freedom. I was spending little time at home; I was only there to shower and sleep. Because I was travelling over 4 hours a day to and from work, I ate on the go. This worked out brilliantly for me and I could plan my meals around my jogs. I was totally obsessed.

Five months had passed and I had lost just over 4 stone. I had gone down 6 trouser sizes but I still didn't look like the runners in the magazines I was reading. I had to start doing strength and conditioning work to minimise the chances of me getting injured so I plucked up the courage to join a gym that was close to the train station. My plan was to go straight after work and, thank God that I joined the one that I did. It was almost as if I the universe had intended all along for me to join this one as I met a personal trainer there called Eddie. He had personal experience at competing to a professional level when he was younger. Plus, it helped that he was softly spoken and a lot shorter than me; I didn't feel threatened or intimidated in any way.

Eddie and I worked together a couple of times a week for the next 5 months. He kept trying to encourage me to join a running club but, in my mind, I wasn't good enough. Eddie was a great trainer; he never raised his voice and was always calm and supportive, which is exactly the kind of personality I needed. We were the perfect fit.

I think one of the reasons we got on so well was because I coped well with pain. I got my head down and took my mind to a different place – a skill that I had mastered as a child.

One day, and rather unexpectedly, Eddie mentioned that the gym had announced a national competition and the first prize was an all-expenses-paid luxury holiday. He thought I had a good chance of winning. Eddie obviously believed in me more than I did, but I guess that's one of the reasons why I trusted him.

The competition was called *The New You Awards*. I had turned my health around in just 11 months, had lost 8 stone and gone from a weekend shuffler to now running and competing in races. But I still didn't share Ed's confidence and I didn't want to waste anyone's time.

Ed said, very seriously, "Look, you ran a race last weekend and came second out of 600 runners. You can 100% win this!" I agreed. He filled out all the relevant paperwork and sent it off for me, I wasn't so great with identifying my positives.

A couple of weeks had gone by and we hadn't heard anything from them. I was a little relieved. But one evening, after a hard hills session, Ed sat down in the gym talking about my next training phase and what

I needed to expect. Our conversation quickly turned from training to *The New You Awards* and Ed said what a shame it was that we hadn't heard from them, especially as the entry requirements seemed to have been written with me in mind. I guessed it wasn't meant to be.

The next morning I had just gotten back from a run, heading upstairs for a shower, when Mum shouted up. "You have a letter here!" I should have been excited but I had just run 10 miles in the freezing cold and I needed to thaw out! I came downstairs into the kitchen where I found Mum waiting with the letter. I had already convinced myself in the shower that it was a 'sorry, you've not been accepted letter' so I wasn't excited about it.

I opened it to reveal it was a letter inviting Ed and me to London for a posh meal and a stay in an even posher hotel. I knew Ed would be more excited than me. We agreed to go down but I still didn't think I had a chance at placing anywhere in the competition as there were over 10,000 entries. We met the other 11 short-listed candidates at the meal and they all had achieved so much more than I had. It was a loud, busy room, full of people I didn't know. I felt massively exposed and if it hadn't been for Eddie, I would have been on the next train home.

The next day we were up extra early. All 12 of the short-listed candidates had different interviews throughout the day. Then we had to face the judges. I found it all very daunting, opening up and explaining why I had decided to change my life and what my goals and motives were. Even though I was used to having one-to-one conversations with complete strangers in the salon, I really didn't like being interviewed by so many different people and having to explain myself to them all. I wasn't confident and I felt like I was being interrogated. The longer it went on, the more I started to disassociate from the people around me.

Ed could tell I was struggling. We broke for lunch after a gruelling 7 hours. Ed and I went for a short walk so that I could get myself together. "Just think of it as a long hill climb. Take it one step at a time and before you know it, you'll be at the top," Ed said. I'd rather run a hundred hills any day.

During the next phase of the interviews, we had to say which of the other competitors we thought had done well and who we thought should win. There must have been 40 people in that room and I could feel myself beginning to panic; I just didn't cope well in spaces where I felt trapped. Others had slowly started to realise I was panicking. Some tried to reassure me everything was okay, even to compliment me on losing all the weight and that I had inspired them to enter a race. That meant more to me than anything: I had inspired someone to do something that they didn't previously think they could have done

By this point, I was feeling a lot more relaxed as we were talking about running and I felt like I was back in my comfort zone.

It was time for the judges to announce the 4 category winners from the 12 runners-up. There were winners in health, fitness, shape and sports. I had won the sports category and was overwhelmed. It was totally unexpected, and I had never won anything. I remember Ed putting his arm around me as I began to cry and he whispered in my ear. "You're going to win this, Lee. I put an order into the universe last night for you!" I felt a little confused because I had won my category. What else was left?

Just as I thought that the judges lined up at the front of the room and announced my name, Lee Goodrick, as the overall male winner.

I wasn't sure what was happening. Eddie was pushing me to the front and everyone else had turned to me now clapping. By the time I had got to the front I was a total mess. I think at one point I had snotted on to one of the judge's shoulders when they hugged me. Ed and I were shuffled into a taxi and driven across London for a photoshoot with *The Sun* newspaper.

The awards were held in December and by the new year, I had started doing promotional work for the gym which included a TV advertisement. I had to travel down to the New Forest for filming and, because public transport wasn't ideal, I had to rely on my dad to drive me down.

I was anxious about spending that amount of time alone with him, especially as we needed to share a hotel room. Even though nothing had happened for 10 years, I was still uneasy with the situation. Plus, Dad had never driven that far or even seen a motorway with 6 lanes. It was eventful, to say the least! At one point, Dad had missed our junction, panicked, then reversed on the M25!

After the article in *The Sun*, I was starting to be contacted by other newspapers and radio stations to give interviews. They were local and regional which led to me be interviewed by ITV news. A camera crew were going to come to my home to do some filming but I didn't want my dad being involved so Grace very kindly offered to film at hers.

The prize for winning the award was a 5-star, all-expenses-paid holiday, which included helicopter transfers and business class flights. The resort was a spa hotel so a friend and I had treatments daily. It really was like something from the TV that only celebrities go to. My only regret about that holiday was that I took someone who I thought was a friend. Unfortunately, she wasn't and I wish I had listened to my mum and taken Grace instead.

Have you ever experienced disconnecting or dissociation?

What is meant by the term 'dissociation'? This is when our brain and the rest of our nervous system feels overwhelmed with what's going on at that moment. Our brain disconnects us by pulling us away from reality because it's too much for us to manage. It does this to protect us from trauma or pain.

When this is happening, we can feel like we are outside of our body, like we're watching a movie of ourselves. This is known as depersonalisation. De-realisation is where we feel disconnected from our environment. This is a feeling that everything around us doesn't feel real.

People usually have a 'trigger' that brings on dissociating. One of my triggers, for example, is when I am in a small room with other people. Without warning, I can be back to being a child and being restricted by my dad or Alex. A feeling that I can't get away. It can also happen when a man with a deep voice yells, even if he's nowhere near me. For instance, I could be stood waiting for a bus and a complete stranger that's 200 metres away from shouting can still trigger me to dissociate. Instantly, I feel a sense of dread in the pit of my stomach and panic. I immediately have flashbacks to when my dad used to be an inch from my face yelling at me or visions of it happening to my mum and Grace, which still causes me to disconnect from the place I am in.

I used to do everything and anything to avoid small or busy places. It would only take one guy to shout to his dog and I would freeze. Being in a same-sex relationship didn't help either; even though I trusted my partner, as soon as he raised his voice, I'd freak out.

and others, as well as identifying behavioural patterns and how to break them.

Before this, I tried CBT (cognitive behavioural therapy) which I felt was pushing me to deal with problems by trying to alter the way that I think or behave in particular situations. But just because it wasn't right for me, doesn't mean that it won't be for you. Everyone copes and deals with things differently, so always give something a go. You can see how you feel after a session and one type of therapy may be right for you. But you may need to find a different therapist that you connect with better to get the most out of your sessions. Don't forget to check out your therapist's qualifications and ask for a consultation first; these are usually free and it's a great way to know if you will feel relaxed with them.

Sessions can be expensive. Mine cost £90 a week in 2012 and I went for 2 years. Thankfully, I only had myself to support. Depending on where you live, you may qualify for NHS therapies through your doctor or self-referral services but you will need to be ready to tell someone why you need help first, which in itself can be incredibly painful. I hope that the skills to follow give you much-needed relief and support until you feel ready to take steps to therapy. I've developed these from my own experiences and years of research.

How to reconnect and reground

When I first started talking therapy, I really struggled to connect in the sessions whenever the therapist asked me questions about my trauma or the things that had happened in my life to make me to dissociate. At first, it was easy to talk because it was almost like I was explaining someone else's situation rather than my own. Other times, I would have trouble remembering what we had talked about previously or I couldn't speak at all. It was frustrating for me as I just wanted to make progress and not feel like I was wasting my therapist's time.

All these feelings are normal and a high percentage of people in this position have similar experiences. There isn't a right or wrong way to feel. The skills below are what worked for me when I have been in triggering situations and I've needed to reconnect. I've also used the 'Box Breathing' exercise, found at the end of chapter 5.

1. Try and notice objects around you. What colour are they? What shape is the object? Are there any details or patterns on it? This will start to bring your awareness back into the space you are in.

2. How do you feel? Are you hot or cold? Are you hungry or thirsty?

3. What can you hear? Can you hear cars or birds or even a ticking clock?

4. Try wiggling your fingers and toes. Next, move your head from side to side. Can you feel the ground? Notice the pressure under your feet or the chair you're sat in.

Now that you're becoming aware, know that you are in control. You may need to practise these steps 5 or 6 times while you are present in the moment so that you can recall them when you're high or low. Having them stuck on a bathroom mirror or on the inside of a kitchen cupboard can help you to remember the steps too.

5. Keep something small in a coat or trouser pocket or in your bag and, when you feel yourself disconnecting, reach for it and

hold it in your hand. Notice the texture. Is it smooth or rough?

Play with it in your hand, squeeze it, rub it, feel every part of it.

I always have a crystal in my coat pocket, just in case. I have a variety, different shapes, some polished, others not. They can be something special or simply pebbles from the garden. A friend of mine uses an old farthing.

Don't forget to breathe slowly and deeply to make it more powerful. Look into a mirror at your own eyes. I've done this in a coffee shop bathroom and when I've been on a train, I've even used the camera on my phone. Using your pet and looking into their eyes works too.

The more you practice the more you'll become a pro!

You really are amazing and I am with you all the way. You're not alone.

Chapter 3

Trials and Tribulations

'The part of my life when I learnt to fight through the roller coaster of life'

It was the beginning of April and I had just competed in a half marathon in 27-degree heat. The course was particularly hard and hilly and I crossed the finish line in 88 minutes. I remember thinking that this was going to be my best year yet. I was now weighing in at 12 stone; that is a total loss of 11 stone. I had turned myself into a decent runner!

One Saturday afternoon later that month, I arrived home from work to find Mum hunched over in her armchair. I hurried to her and I could hear that she was wheezing. She'd been like this all day and not wanted to bother anyone; she hated a fuss. I grabbed my inhaler and helped her to use it. Within minutes, her breathing had started to become easier. It was the first time I had ever seen Mum this poorly. Although she was a tough lady, she looked scared. It must have been more serious than she was letting on.

Once Mum had calmed down, I managed to get her to eat something. To know that she had been like that all day and not called Grace or me broke my heart but that is how she was. Her kids are the same: we are all stubborn!

The next morning, I was up early for my run with a friend. Mum hadn't slept and was already downstairs, wheezing again but she assured me that she was okay and was just catching her breath. "It must just be a bad chest cold," she said. "You should go on your run. Just leave me that inhaler." My friend was a nurse and she reluctantly agreed with Mum that it wasn't anything to worry about. Mum wasn't just stubborn, she was a nightmare – in the sweetest way possible. She never wanted to be anyone's inconvenience and much preferred to be left alone. And, because she was so good at pretending she was always okay, you wouldn't know if there really was anything to worry about.

Even though I had been reassured Mum would be fine, I couldn't stop thinking of the day before and I cut our run short. I wanted to be at home, just in case she needed something. We'd only been running 20 minutes, if that, and when I got back home, she wasn't wheezing but her skin had changed to an ash colour.

Immediately, I rang Grace and explained how Mum was. She told me not to worry. "Mum will be fine your probably overreacting." But I insisted that Grace came over and check on her and she drove up with her friend. They were in the middle of having a BBQ and, to their mind, I was overreacting. Mum was *always* fine!

Once she arrived, Grace said Mum probably had a bad chest infection and told me not to worry. Maybe she would be fine so I may as well finish off my run. Once I had left, Grace and her friend popped Mum into the car and took her to our local hospital just to get her checked over.

Later that evening, as I got back, nobody was home. Grace had left a note on the kitchen table telling me they had gone to the hospital so at least I knew where they were. This was before mobiles phones so I had no way of contacting anyone. I just prayed that everything was okay and guessed they were probably still waiting to be seen.

Grace called a few hours later and said that Mum had been checked over. "They have done a few scans," Grace said, "Lee, it's not good news."

The doctors had discovered that Mum was in the late stages of heart failure. My heart dropped into the pit of my stomach and all it felt like all time had stopped. I left that phone call not knowing which way was up or down.

There is a history of early deaths due to cardiovascular disease on Mum's side of the family. Both of her parents died before the age of 66 and Mum had always said that if she could make it to 67 then she was safe. She was fast approaching that birthday and she just needed to get over this little issue and then everything would be okay. They had a short wait in the emergency department for a bed on the cardiac ward so Mum can be transferred up for specialist care

It was now Tuesday and Grace had come to pick me up so we could visit Mum on the ward. One of my brothers and his wife were already there. We all sat around her bed, not really knowing what to say or do. Mum turned to look over at Grace and then said, sharply, "Grace." And then Mum began to go into cardiac arrest.

A team of medics came running into the room and we were all shuffled into the relative's room at the end of the ward. Everyone sat around, hugging and crying while I was stood alone, looking out of the window.

I felt totally numb and, like other times when I felt terrified, I began to disconnect from my environment.

One of the doctors came in to speak to us. They'd found a weak pulse and, like a bullet, I was off straight to my Mum's bed. The curtains where drawn. I was expecting to see her hooked up to a life support machine like you see on TV.

Instead, there nothing. She was laying super-still, with her head back and her mouth open. I noticed that her hair had been messed up and then I glanced over to her arm, covered in blood. She's not going to be happy with that, I thought. Messy hair and blood on her arm really wasn't going to impress her. Rather than hugging her or saying goodbye, I reached over for a pack of wet wipes and started to clean her arm and I tried to fix her hair.

It's crazy what the mind does when it's under massive amounts of stress and pain.

My siblings arranged everything for the funeral and wake because I was in a world of my own. When anyone spoke to me it sounded like they were under water; my body was running on autopilot.

Back at home, it was weird like Mum had gone on holiday and not told anyone that she was going. Everything was still immaculate just as she had left it. Grace very kindly let me and Poky, the incredibly old family dog, live with her until things had settled. But it wasn't long before Poky took ill like he was pining after Mum. His kidneys had failed and the vet suggested that we put him to sleep. I couldn't cope with taking him so Grace and her husband took him for me. I remember standing in their lounge watching him go to the vets and again I was numb. It just reinforced my disconnection from what I was already going through.

When they brought Poky back, I took him home to bury him in our back garden. This was the first time I had seen Dad in weeks. He wasn't welcome at the funeral because of everything he had put Mum through and, if he had shown up, my brothers would have most probably killed him. I think we all blamed him for weakening Mum's heart.

In the space of a couple of months, I had lost everything: my Mum, my home and my dog. But I still hadn't shed a tear. Instead of crying, I felt anger and frustration towards myself for not reacting as others expected me too. It reaffirmed my feelings that there was something wrong with me. I was feeling anger towards Mum for leaving me and frustration with myself because I wasn't strong enough to say goodbye. I felt shame, too, for not allowing my dad to say his goodbye to her either. They must have loved each other at some point. Why else would they have married?

Instead of me using my running or something else healthy to vent, I took my feelings out on Grace. It wasn't until years later – looking back on those times – that I realised just how much she must have loved me. Nobody can turn back time; I just had to make sure to never treat anyone else like I had treated her. Especially as she was suffering too, after all the months of despair and emotional torment.

I had started to get crippling stomach pains and my bowel motions had become erratic. At the time, I put it down to stress or something I had eaten. I wasn't running much after Mum's death but I continued to lose weight.

A couple of weeks later, I went to my doctor. They ran a few tests: my bloods were a little out of sorts and I had some biomarkers so she sent me to the hospital for more tests. It wasn't long before the results were back. Grace had come with me. She said, when I came out, that she knew something was wrong, I had been in there for a long time.

Grace turned to me and asked me what the doctor had said. "They said I have a tumour in my colon but it's been caught early. They need to schedule me in for surgery to remove the small growth then assess things for oncology appointments." After they had removed the growth, they wanted me to start 3 months of chemotherapy.

When they hear the word 'chemo', people think you'll lose all your hair, be constantly vomiting and have massive weight loss. But this wasn't the case for me. I slammed on the weight. I was popping 8 steroid pills a day and enough anti-sickness tablets to sink a ship. The chemo came in the form of a pill that I took for 14 days and then had 2 days off, repeating this cycle 5 times.

I told you I was lucky. Whenever I see others going through their diagnosis I can't help but thank God for saving me from all that anguish. It was as if He was giving me a break from any more suffering.

In the following month after finishing treatment, I slowly began to get my life back on track. I had started jogging again; it was tough. I felt like I had my life going smoothly. I had just started seeing someone. The universe was looking out for me.

Chapter 4

Letting Go

'Where I learnt that if I couldn't change my circumstances, I could change how I see and react to them'

F ast forward 8 years and I was still in remission. Everything was going blissfully and I had just turned 34. My doctor was treating me for IBS (irritable bowel syndrome) but no matter what I took or the different dietary changes I made, I was constantly on the toilet. If I didn't eat anything, I relief while they ran yet more tests. One of which was a capsule endoscopy (the capsule you swallow contains a camera that takes images of the gastrointestinal tract, the images are then sent wirelessly to a recorder for a doctor to view later) and that same day I had biopsies taken from my large bowel as the capsule had shown cobble-stoning. This was, in fact, blisters and it gave the doctors more information about how to focus treatment and gave them a better idea of what to look for in my blood.

One new blood test showed elevated C-reactive protein markers (these are an indicator of inflammation within the body). My levels were at 228. To put that into perspective, a healthy person's level would be around 0.4! They needed to get my markers down, so I was started on a powerful steroid given directly into the vein. would still need to open my bowels a couple of times a day. If I dare to eat anything at all then I may as well set up camp in the bathroom!

As I could be on the toilet for 8 hours or more, I had every test possible. Still nothing showed up as abnormal. This went on for over a year until my doctor finally admitted me into hospital. After some blood tests came back showing that my electrolytes were down and I was severely dehydrated, I then spent 3 weeks in hospital while they treated me for pain and gave me symptomatic

I had this 3 times a day for 2 weeks.

My bowel had been so inflamed that I couldn't digest food properly and needed to be fed by a tube. Thankfully, once the steroids had kicked in, the tube could be removed but I would still be on liquid meals for a month or so after I had returned home, just to help me regain some weight.

After another year of being in and out of hospital, I was diagnosed with Crohn's colitis disease. This is an autoimmune condition that's incredibly hard to diagnose, which is why it had taken so long. The immune system attacks the lining of the bowel, like it is a foreign body, resulting in inflammation and blisters forming in the bowel and colon. It's very painful but, once diagnosed, preventative treatments can be started.

The tricky part is finding a drug that works and does not cause too many side effects. For the next few years, Crohn's didn't allow me to work full-time, sometimes not at all, so I relied heavily on state benefits. My mental health also struggled as I had always worked and I felt ashamed. I wasn't used to handouts but I didn't have enough money to cover my bills. Along with trying to manage the symptoms of the disease, I struggled immensely with fatigue, partly because my body was not able to absorb nutrients from my food.

I was still constantly on the toilet. I was on the maximum dose of a drug called loperamide and I was on a lot of morphine for the horrendous cramps. Most days they were so painful that I didn't know what to do with myself; any position I tried did nothing to alleviate the pain.

I was also catheterised which led to a never-ending cycle of inflammatory flare-ups, infections and other side effects. But finally, I managed to get on top of it all. It was a huge adjustment and I had to get used to carrying around a spare pair of pants, baby wipes and anything else I needed in case I had an accident and couldn't get to a toilet fast enough. If I thought I needed to pass wind, by the time I had realised it was too late and I would be sat on public transport on the way to work with soiled pants.

A lady I used to work with had started her own salon in the small village where she had grown up. She knew about my health but still kindly offered me a position to be a self-employed stylist. It was perfect; I could do as many hours as I could manage and it got me off benefits. We got on great and she is such a beautiful soul and an exceptionally talented stylist. I massively looked up to her and I truly felt blessed. Even though I sometimes fell ill at work, at times needing an ambulance, none of that phased her or our clients. On my good days, we had a brilliant laugh and it was a great place to be.

***

About this time, I heard from an old neighbour, who still lived next door to my dad. After Mum's death, my dad had a massive breakdown. He had been living in Mum's house since her death 9 years ago but he had destroyed to the point that it was unrecognisable. I had not seen him in 6 years because I found it too painful. The neighbour was calling me to tell me that he had been causing trouble on the street and some kids had thrown bricks through the windows. She said she didn't know who else to contact as everyone had washed their hands of him.

When I arrived, I struggled to gain access to the house. He had built barricades against the broken windows and the front door. The only way I could get in was to squeeze down the side of the house, over debris and more barricades. The back of the house was just as bad: he had boarded everything up but there was a small opening at the bottom of the back door that I could climb through. I guessed this was how he was getting in and out.

Inside, it was dark and cold. I tried the light switches but either the bulbs had fused or the electricity had been cut off. I could just make out where was clear to step. He had become a hoarder and there wasn't one space that wasn't filled with something: rotten food was left out, broken glass all over the floors, it stank of urine and it was that cold inside I could see my breath.

Going through everything downstairs had woken Dad up. He had been napping in one of the bedrooms and, when he came downstairs, he wasn't happy to see me. I had absolutely no idea what to do and I was still very much scared of him. But he needed help. I was the only one he had.

I rang a close friend and she recommended that I call the police. They came out with an on-call doctor as Dad was extremely aggressive and risked causing harm to himself and others. They made the decision to section him under the mental health act and he was taken to a unit to be assessed. He was admitted and would be held there for a minimum of 28 days.

I had to return to the house to collect his clothes and toiletries. He hardly had anything; the things he did have were soiled. Rather than trying to clean them, it was easier to buy everything new or, as I was struggling to get by myself, from a charity shop.

Work had started to pick up, which brought in much-needed money. It was a blessing as I needed the money for travelling to and from the hospital and to keep Dad stocked. After the 28 days, I had a meeting with Dad's care team to discuss what they had decided was best for him. He was still very volatile and had deep-rooted issues. Dad was in total denial: he had never thought that there was anything ever wrong with him and he blamed everyone else.

They re-sectioned him, this time for 6 months which he absolutely needed. It meant that he received medication to help manage his condition. There was also talking therapy which he must have struggled with. After he had been discharged, Dad needed extended care and a community treatment order (CTO) was put into place to make sure he didn't relapse. It was decided that Mum's house wasn't suitable for him to go back to, which is understandable, and I was not in any position to be able to fix it, so the CTO had moved him to a 'safe' bungalow away from the old house and away from the kids that had tormented him. I'm sure Dad wasn't an innocent party but later I learnt the kids had been stealing from the house too.

I managed to sort a few pieces of furniture to be taken from Mum's to his new home. Because of the medication, he struggled to care for himself and so carers came 3 times a day. He refused to see them and wouldn't let them in. Again, I had no other choice to step up; he was still my dad, whether I liked it or not. He had nobody else other than me.

Mum had tried multiple times to get him help over the years. The doctor had said that Dad had a personality disorder and that there wasn't any treatment he could offer. I guess, for years, and even before he got together with Mum, Dad had developed skills to cope and hide what was really going on.

Now that Dad had an assigned social worker to look out for his wellbeing, and she knew parts of his history that had been documented, she was in contact with me to keep me up to date with how he was doing. She knew a little about the emotional abuse he put his family through and could understand why I found it difficult to be around him but she didn't know about the sexual abuse – I wasn't going tell her, it had nothing to with my dad's care and I wasn't one for airing my dirty washing out for the world to see.

After a while, she rang to tell me that she was concerned that Dad wasn't eating properly, nor seemed to be washing. The medication was making him very unsteady on his feet and quite spaced out most of the time. He was a shadow of his former self and no longer was the man I was terrified of. He had turned into a frail old man that shuffled along and, because of this, I made the commitment to visit once a week and care for him as much as I could.

It was a 30-mile round trip to his and back. I could spend around 5 hours cleaning from top to bottom as he couldn't do anything himself. I had to do his food shopping, which took time as I was still relying on public transport. But then there was the part that I dreaded the most: his shower.

I tried my hardest to not think about it but it was on my mind for days leading up to me going over. It would make me physically sick but it needed doing – he was now incontinent – and there wasn't anyone else to sort him out. We hardly spoke; I just wanted to get there, get it done and leave. I think he knew that.

This went on for 2 years.

How could I care for a man that had hurt me, Mum and Grace in so many ways? Well, it was as simple as *forgiveness*. I couldn't change the things that had happened, nor could I understand why they did happen. But the one thing that I could control was my own feelings towards him. I had a choice: I could either carry all the hate and resentment with me for the rest of my life or I could choose to let it go.

A great man once said, "Holding onto anger is like drinking poison and expecting the other person to die." [Buddha]

Forgiveness is a choice. You are in control of how your emotions affect you. I was no longer willing to allow my abuser to have that power over me – so I let it all go. It sounds simple because it is. But just because you're forgiving someone, doesn't mean that you understand why it happened or why it was you and not somebody else. It took me years to let go of all that hate and pain but I needed to as I couldn't let it keep affecting everything I did. The pain I carried with me daily impacted my relationships and, even 20 years later I would still have nightmares about it.

But how did I know it was the right time for me to be able to let go?

Forgiveness is a gift that you are giving yourself. It allows you to let go of that voice in your head that follows you everywhere, no matter what you are doing. It doesn't matter what type of trauma you have suffered, your abuser has weakened and confused you and they will steal your connection to yourself and the people that you love. Slowly, over time, everything becomes tiny and you may find yourself in a position where you are alone and have become isolated from the world.

One day, you'll realise that you have the choice to take your power back. You have a choice to either let the mental hurt carry on or to put an end to it and take back your power and strength.

I know how incredibly hard it is to even think that you can be emotionally free. But I believe in you and I know that you are ready to break free because you're reading this. In the next chapter, we'll look at the skill I used to finally let go. I am with you every step of the way. Read through it a few times until you are ready.

Chapter 5

The Forgiveness Skill

'Just because you forgive does not mean you accept the evil'.

To let it all go – the pain, the hurt, the anger – you must be ready to give this skill everything you've got. This isn't going to be easy. It may even take you several attempts to get all your feelings out.

Remember, you are doing this for *you* and nobody else.

When you're ready, you'll need the following:

    1. Something to write a letter on

    2. A box of tissues

    3. Plenty of time

    4. Self-love

If you're struggling with finding self-love, think of the universe or a higher power sending you all the love you deserve. And remember, you are doing this so that you can love yourself again.

This skill can either help you to forgive yourself for hanging onto your past or to forgive that person who hurt you. This letter has been created by using some techniques used in cognitive behavioural therapy (CBT) and refined during the years of my own therapy.

How to write a letter:

Dear …,

You have …

First, tell them in as much detail as possible what they have done to you.

This has made me feel …

The more connected you feel to your emotions, the greater the freedom you'll feel at the end of this.

What you did has impacted my life …

Explain how their actions have affected your life.

I have chosen to forgive you because …

It's important to completely let go of everything and free yourself from the emotional weight on your shoulders.

Signed …

If you're struggling to find the words or you're feeling lost, here is the letter I wrote:

Dear Dad,

You took my innocence and it wasn't yours to take. You hurt me so deeply and hurt me in every way possible. When you should have been protecting, loving and nurturing me as I grew, you instead forced yourself onto me physically and hurt me emotionally. It was going to affect me for the rest of my life. I would never trust a man ever again. I would never know honest affection.

You didn't just destroy my childhood, you obliterated any chance of me having a sexual relationship. And, because of you, I've had a life terrified of being in small spaces with others. If a man raises his voice on TV, it immediately takes me back to the times that you were loud and aggressive to me and the ones I loved.

You made me feel worthless to the point that I only felt safe in abusive relationships or being around toxic people because I knew what to expect from them. It's the only way I knew how to interact with anyone.

I am no longer letting you continue to hurt me and I am taking full control of my emotions and thinking patterns to only allow positives into my life!

I am a strong, confident person that chooses to let go of the shame and anger I feel towards you.

I am sending you kind thoughts and love.

I forgive you.

Lee Goodrick 01.11.16

Your letter may take several attempts to write down all your feelings and that's okay. It took me 5 goes to finally get everything out that I wanted.

You may need to collect your thoughts after revisiting traumatic memories. It can often leave us feeling disconnected and unable to communicate with others. To reconnect to the present, we need to calm and slow everything down and make sure we're getting enough oxygen: sometimes we can forget to breathe when we disconnect as we can become lost in the moment. At other times, we can breathe too fast and hard, like we are in fight or flight mode. The next skill will help you to feel in control again.

Remember you are strong and brave; you are doing amazing!

Box Breathing

Often, after therapy sessions, I was left feeling disconnected from myself and the world around me. I felt in a bubble. My sessions were held in the town centre and I could easily feel confused and scared afterwards. I would endlessly walk around, not knowing what I was doing or where I was going. 'Box Breathing' is an amazing skill to have and will help you in any situation, either to prepare you for challenging times or to help you take stock after them.

How to do 'Box Breathing':

1. Start by sitting or lying down, whichever is most comfortable for you. You can choose to keep your eyes open or gently close them, do whatever feels safe for you.

2. Take a slow, deep breath in for a count of 4.

3. Hold that breath for a count of 4.

4. Now breathe out for a count of 4.

5. Wait for 4 counts before repeating steps 2–5.

Do this at least 5 times; longer if needed.

If, after doing this, you're feeling low, maybe put on your favourite music, sing and dance along; it's the fastest way to shift your emotions.

Be proud of your achievements. Remember, even if it takes you several goes to write your letter or to grasp the breathing exercise, simply going through the steps will have a positive impact on your life. You might not feel it working straight away but the more you do it, the more embedded it will be in your mind.

Now it's time to be kind to yourself and celebrate what you have achieved. Do whatever makes you feel loved and will recharge your soul. It could be spending time with your pet or being present with your kids. Personally, I reward myself with a pamper night, a movie that'll make me laugh or by buying a piece of clothing that I've wanted for a while but didn't have a reason to have it. Well, *this is that reason.*

Calming anxiety and reconnecting

The breathing skill we've just looked at is used in some extremely volatile and highly stressful situations to calm and control your fight or flight reaction.

If you've ever wondered how a firefighter has the courage to go into a burning building, you can bet they've used 'Box Breathing' to control their fears and overcome their body's natural response. They are in full control in the midst of a terrifying situation. Of course, they're trained for these situations but if they let their emotions take over, all that training is out the window!

Our bodies react to what's going on in the mind. Whether it's a real threat to your life or it's all in your head, the brain can't tell the difference.

A belief doesn't need to be factual: if you believe it to be real then, as far as your mind is concerned, it is. That's why the armed forces and high-performance athletes use similar techniques when they need to control their stress levels. But you don't need to be in a 'risky' or high-pressure situation for this to work; it helps to calm all stresses down, no matter where they are coming from and you can do 'Box Breathing' no matter where you are.

The technique is so powerful that it helped me to come off anxiety medications, which felt amazing. The beta blockers controlled the severity of my panic attacks but they also made me feel spaced out all the time. I had no control over being connected, which I hated, but they gave me a semi-normal life back. It got to the point, 10 years ago, where I couldn't leave my apartment; even taking the rubbish to the bin used to fill me with dread. But once I learnt how to control my breathing, it allowed me to stop taking them.

I remember once out shopping with a friend when a man came too close to me. I started to panic; my anxiety was starting to take control. I began sweating – even though it was freezing cold. The sweat was dripping off me and I could feel others starting to look. I found a quiet spot at the back of the supermarket and started to 'Box Breathe' and within 30 seconds my heart had stopped racing. I was becoming more aware of objects around me and a moment later, the sweating had stopped. I was now fully present and got back to what I was doing before it had started.

Always speak to your doctor before you try alternatives. Please do not take yourself off medication without speaking to a doctor or nurse.

Chapter 6

Testing Days

'The darkest time of my life'

Dad's social worker called unexpectedly. She wanted to make sure that the hospital had been in touch but I had no idea what she was talking about. She filled me in: Dad had decided that he needed to go into the bank and he had slipped on the steps and banged his head quite badly. An ambulance had taken him to hospital to get checked over.

At this point, I was living 90 miles away. Luckily, I now had my driving licence and was still going over every Sunday to see him and get the jobs done. His accident happened in the middle of the week. Normally, he would have waited for me to take him; but recently Dad had become confused, mostly down to the mixture of medication and old age. I didn't think it was anything to worry about or I would have taken him to see his doctor. I had spoken with his social worker and she just confirmed it was normal.

When I finally got in touch with the hospital, the doctor looking after him asked me if I could be with him. They were running a series of tests and Dad was getting anxious as he didn't understand what was going on. I sorted out my shifts at work and left straight away. A few hours later, at the hospital, the doctor greeted me, the test results were back and it was not good news.

Dad looked in a daze. He was more confused than usual. A team of people came to see us both; they looked at me and said maybe I'd like to hold dad's hand. "We have the results of your scans, Mr Goodrick and I am sorry to say the tests show you have stage 4 lung cancer. It has metastasised to your brain and, unfortunately, there isn't anything we can do, it will just be a matter of managing your symptoms."

I don't think Dad totally understood what was being said. He just heard the 'C-word' and started to cry. The doctor carried on saying that he was going to fast-track palliative care and that he gave Dad around 6 weeks to live. Even though Dad needed me more than ever, I still struggled to put my arms around to comfort him; just because I had forgiven him, didn't mean that I had forgotten about everything that had happened. I was still going to be there for him, but not in the way that others around us would have expected me to be with him. Our relationship had nothing to do with anyone else. My dad had my love and support; that's all that mattered.

My head went into overdrive. I needed to find a nursing home that could take him as soon as possible. I had no idea where to start. Sara, a close friend, asked me if I needed any help. I asked if she would mind coming with me to look around care homes as I had no idea what to expect and I wasn't sure what I was looking for. I knew it had to be able to give the medical care he needed but I also wanted something that he would feel comfortable in too.

Together, we found a beautiful home that overlooked a country park and it wasn't that far from where he had been living. The staff were great and they sorted out the hospital transfers. I didn't need to do anything other than just spend time with him. I would have liked to have found a home closer to where I was living but the accents would have only confused him more – they confused me most of the time – so he would have had no chance! The last thing I wanted was to put him in a stressful situation if it wasn't necessary. He was still my dad. If I hadn't forgiven him years ago, he would have been in this situation alone. Thinking of anybody going through the end of their life alone breaks my heart.

While all this was happening, I was in a relationship. However, things were not so great between my partner Chris and me. He was a kind person, but I had anxiety issues mostly caused by my Crohn's and I had moved to a new city, miles away. I didn't know anybody and, in my first year there, I was housebound. We were completely different people but I didn't realise this until we had moved in together. I was at home 24/7 and he liked to go out with his friends; I didn't mind as I didn't want him to suffer because I was ill but it eventually started to strain our relationship. We drifted further and further apart.

Chris was brilliant for me while Dad was dying. He supported me financially, which allowed me to go part-time at work and meant I could spend more travelling down to spend time with Dad. He was receiving fantastic care but I knew that, at some point, he would be alone in his room and I knew what feeling scared and alone feels like. I made it my priority to spend as much time as I could with him. Two wrongs don't make a right; I had the choice to let him suffer but I'm not that kind of person.

***

Over the next few weeks, I was driving down as much as I could. I had only been driving a year and had gone from 30 miles a week to now over 600. Motorway driving wasn't great at the best of times, especially when I was feeling so overwhelmed. With all the added stress, I couldn't sleep and was struggling to eat too. I was suffering with anxiety, trying to hold a broken relationship together and still work a job that needed me to be constantly happy.

Both my boss and clients knew what was happening and it was nice while I was at work: I could forget about things for a while. Increasingly, I was finding it hard to concentrate so I went to my doctor to explain my situation. She prescribed me beta blockers; they were incredible. She also gave me a short course of sleeping tablets and asked me if I wanted an increased dose of the anti-depressants. I had started them after Mum died and was already taking a big dose, so I declined the offer – I hated taking medication.

Just as I thought things were going okay, Dad's condition took a turn and he was now going downhill fast. I felt out of control and my stress levels were through the roof. My Crohn's had started to flare up and I managed as well as I could have until I needed to seek medical help. My doctor sent me to have blood work done to see what my CRP (C-reactive protein markers) levels were. The results came back showing them at 106, which meant I was definitely having a flare-up. I needed an increase in morphine to manage the pain and it helped to slow down the bowel.

I couldn't take the morphine while I was travelling; I could only take it when I had enough time for it to leave my system before I drove, meaning I had to have a clear 8 hours. I had just started taking a week's worth of steroids to try and control my CRP. I needed those to work fast – there was no way I could be admitted to hospital as Dad didn't have long. I'd need to be at his side so I couldn't be hooked up to a drip.

Chris's mum, Mary, gave me massive amounts of support. She had been a nurse and is an amazing woman: the things that she's seen and been through over the years had made her into a tough cookie. At one point, she worked as a Marie Curie nurse. I looked up to her and if angels exist – she must be one. I have never known someone so good at everything, even at colouring her own hair, she never missed a spot!

It was now the first week in September and it had been 5 weeks since Dad's diagnosis. He was now struggling to swallow thickened liquids and he could only manage to mumble a few words. I didn't care that I couldn't understand what he was saying, I just took it as a reassurance that he knew I was there and that he knew he wasn't alone. Mary had prepared me for what was about to come. She knew I couldn't handle any more surprises.

In the days to come, I didn't leave his side. His skin had started to change colour and his fingers and toes were becoming greyish-blue and, no matter how much I turned the heat up in his room, he was always cold. I knew then that this was his body beginning to die. His breathing had started to become more erratic: fast then slow. At times it sounded like he was holding his breath. I knew why this was happening, Mary had told me all about it.

The doctor had given the order to hook up the morphine pump. Once the pump goes in, it's 'normally' only a few hours until the end. But Dad hung in. He wasn't quite ready to leave just yet. It felt like he had one foot in this world and one in the next.

Sara didn't live far from the care home and had driven over to support me. We had only been friends for a couple of years. I had met her in the village salon I used to work at. She used to go to one of the other stylists but, for whatever reason, came to me. We got on well and she had a crazy sense of humour and so did her husband. To me, they felt more like family. It was as if the universe had brought them into my life for a reason other than a haircut. I would have done anything for them: if she needed a kidney then I would have been straight there.

Until she arrived, I felt like I was treading water in a deep ocean, just about managing to keep my head from going under while waiting for a tidal wave to take me. Sara gave the best hugs and, for a split second, I'd forgotten what was happening. I can't remember how long Sara stayed with us but she came straight from work and left the next day. It can't have been easy for her to sit in that room. Those last few hours of waiting for the end were horrendous.

Dad was exactly like I had seen Mum laying all those years ago. It's not easy to forget. His skin was grey and waxy, his head was back and his mouth was now open constantly. I could see into his mouth and it shocked me that even his mouth had turned black. I knew then that he was breathing so hard because it was his body fighting to survive. He was completely asleep, free of any pain.

I didn't know where to look. Sara suggested that I stroke his head and hold his hand as these are the last senses to go so I could still let him know I was there. His passing was close. His breathing had changed again, it was now fast and deep with long periods of holding his breath. I remember Mary telling me that this was when carbon dioxide builds up in the brain. Every now and again the nurse on duty would pop in to check on him. She encouraged me to take a break, to have a coffee or something to eat, but I wasn't with Mum when she passed and there was no way I was leaving him.

I put on the music that he used to enjoy. For me, that brought back memories – some good but mostly bad. But this wasn't about me. I hoped it may have settled him a little. The nurse came in, put her hand on my shoulder and said it would only be an hour or so. As she left, I felt dread in my heart. I started to sob.

And I began to pray. I prayed for him. I prayed with every inch of my being.

I was still stroking his head when it felt like time had stopped. I couldn't hear his breathing or the music anymore. I opened my eyes and could still see his chest moving up and down. I shut my eyes again and totally let go. I imagined ripples emerging from my body. I was still praying, still sobbing. A faint but clear whisper in my ear said "forgive me". Out loud, I said, "Dad, I love you and I forgive you." Then, he was gone.

I could hear the music again. I never did tell him I had written that letter of forgiveness.

I wouldn't say I was a 'full-blown' Christian but I know that there is a higher place, whether that be the universe, a God or something else. There have been times in my life that I have prayed to a higher power and things that I have needed have been brought into my life: people or situations to teach me something. The only thing I know for certain is that everything that exists is energy and that energy cannot be destroyed. It will always be so we will never really die. Both my parents were atheists but, when they both passed, their 'being' or 'soul' has gone somewhere. The body left behind is only a shell.

Dad's funeral wasn't straightforward. Because he had been a coal miner since he was 13, the coroner needed to be involved and a formal inquest was needed. They needed to know whether the lung cancer was down to industrial diseases or because Dad had been a smoker. Until a decision had been made on the cause of his death, nothing could be written on a death certificate. This meant I couldn't sort out his affairs either. While dad was alive, I had power of attorney but this ended when he died.

***

I couldn't do anything for the next 6 weeks so, reluctantly, I allowed my doctor to admit me to hospital to get my flare-ups under control. I was reluctant because 9 times out of 10, with Crohn's, you're put in a side room and you're alone for much of your stay. A side room was great as you had your own toilet but, other than that, it was deadly quiet and so far, I had managed to avoid thinking about what I had just been through

…

I was in that bed for 2 long weeks with nothing else to do but think.

Mary was kind enough to visit nearly every day, which took my mind off for a bit. She really is an angel.

When I came out of hospital, I went straight back to normal as if the past 8 weeks had never happened. Work was a great distraction and I practically had the house to myself: Chris was out a lot each night. I had nothing to do so I'd have an extra-large gin (or 5) to help me to relax and sleep. I didn't know at the time, but this would turn into a very slippery slope.

During the day, I had distractions but, at night, I was having trouble sleeping. There was nothing other than my thoughts. I'd convinced my doctor to renew my prescription for sleeping tablets. I discovered that I could get rid of a few days simply by sleeping through them: with a couple of sleepers and a bottle of gin (this wasn't sleep, I was passing out).

At the time, I thought it was great. The coroners were in contact most days, asking for additional information or to inform me of what stage they were at. It was a living nightmare and was causing massive amounts of stress and anxiety; I just wanted to move on but couldn't.

While looking for painkillers for a migraine that I couldn't shift, I opened one of the drawers in the bathroom (one that I hardly ever opened). I had been driving so much to and from Dad's that I hadn't

93

been taking all of my medication, particularly the ones that clouded my judgement. This meant that I had, unknowingly, stockpiled and they were now sitting in that draw, untouched. I should have collected them up and thrown them but, for whatever reason, I didn't. I closed the drawer and carried on with my day, not giving it another thought. There was a mix of morphine, muscle relaxants and nerve pain inhibitors ... a deadly drawer!

Finally, Dad's body had been released by the coroners and now I could get some closure. I made an appointment with a local funeral director. I tried to put a small playlist of songs together for his service but as I played the music, images of my childhood and Dad's passing all came flooding back. I kept thinking about his breathing: I could hear it again like I was reliving that night.

It wasn't until I was sat in the funeral director's office and we were talking about Dad's wishes that I realised he had nobody other than me. It seemed pointless to have a full service and because neither Dad nor I had any savings, I had to rely on a state-funded funeral. I knew from talking to the director that they had limited funds, so I decided to have

Dad cremated and save the crematorium some vital funds for the next family needing their help.

When Dad could make his own decisions, we had spoken about what he wanted at his funeral. Because of everything that had happened over the years, Dad's side of the family had disowned him. I asked him if he wanted me to contact them so that they could attend his funeral but Dad made it very clear that he wanted them to be kept out of it.

Chris had come with me for support when I went to pick up Dad's ashes. On the drive down, we talked about what I should do with them. I told Chris that when I had spoken to Dad about his wishes, he had wanted to be buried with Mum. The night when Dad was struggling to pass, I told him that I would make sure that I lay him with Mum. I have to admit that this was a lie.

I have no doubt that Dad loved Mum. And in the early days, she loved him too. But after everything there was no way I could: he put her through hell when she was alive. She deserved to rest now and, besides, I didn't have the strength to ask her family for permission. Instead, I found a beautiful spot under a tree in the grounds of the crematorium. Autumn sunbeams breaking through the trees guided me to the spot.

We spent a while just sitting and taking in the air before Chris and I drove back. We arrived home earlier than expected so Chris went to see his friends and I opened a bottle of wine. I wished I wasn't alone but, at the same time, I couldn't blame anyone for not wanting to spend time with me. I had become emotionally unpredictable and people didn't know what to do for the best, so they stayed away. I muddled my way through with work and my new best friend: gin.

Gin was there for me no matter what mood I was in. It would never judge me or offer me advice that I didn't want to hear. Gin didn't get offended when I was in a vile mood because I was alone, isolated and scared of the person I was becoming ... a drunk.

Everything would be okay. I just needed another gin to forget about it. There was never any judgement about drinking on a night. After all, everyone at work would say "I can't wait till home time and I can have a drink." It was the norm. Chris binged on a Saturday night with his friends, which wrote off Sundays. But he wouldn't drink through the week.

Alcohol can bring people together or isolate you to the point of no longer wanting to exist. It can give you courage or destroy everything. It's cheap yet it can be so costly to our physical and mental health. Alcohol gave me something to look forward to at the end of the day. No matter how I was feeling if I drank enough everything would melt away.

22nd December

I had finished work for the Christmas break and was looking forward to getting home. A client had brought me a big bottle of gin and the boss had given everyone a bottle of champagne. For the first time in a long while, I was looking forward to seeing Chris. But when I arrived home, he was packing his overnight bag.

He had arranged to spend a night with a group of his friends that weekend so it meant another weekend alone for me. He was finishing up packing when I cracked open the gin. I'd had a particularly hard week at work. I was physically exhausted and emotionally drained too; clients loved to talk about how their Christmases were going to be amazing and that felt unbearable at times.

I had tried to talk to Chris about the last few months and everything that I had gone through. But his response to everything was that "you'll get over it". He wasn't the best at anything emotional and we were only friends now: our relationship had ended just before Dad had gotten ill. What more could I have expected from Chris?

With the house to myself again, the gin wasn't touching the sides. I poured an extra-large measure into a wine glass and then topped it up with the champagne. Halfway through and I could already feel it beginning to kick in. Great, I thought, while Chris is away I'll sleep for a few days.

I went to the drawer in the bathroom and took everything out, put them on the kitchen table and popped them all out of the blister packs. My gin cocktail was nearly gone so I poured the rest of the gin into my glass and began to drink as I grabbed handfuls of the pills and shovelled them into my mouth, making sure I chewed before washing them down with neat gin.

I'd had enough of the hurting and suffering, just to do it all again the next day. I wasn't thinking of anyone. I didn't want to exist. I needed to make sure that I took everything; I needed my life to end. I sobbed, how had my life got to this point?

***

I woke up in hospital. Chris was sitting next to my bed. The first feeling I had was anger: it hadn't worked.

Chris had forgotten his phone charger so had come back in the early hours of the morning (probably hoping I was asleep) and had found me naked on the kitchen floor. He'd managed to get my heart beating and was able to make me vomit then rang for an ambulance. I was hooked up to an ECG monitor and a drip to administer a drug to reverse the effects of the opioids I'd taken.

The doctors told me I was lucky to be here. I had crashed twice and they had to revive me. I didn't feel lucky; I felt so angry that they didn't let me die.

My chest was so sore it felt like I'd been in a fight. The doctor explained this was the effect of needing to do chest compressions. I had a huge bruise that went from just below my right hip down to my knee. Chris said that the table was halfway across the kitchen and he thought I must have hit it when I passed out.

When you've attempted suicide, you stay in hospital until you're physically stable, then they send you home. Then the crisis team (the crisis resolution and home treatment team) can support you if you have a mental health crisis outside of hospital. They follow up with daily visits to your home to assess your mental state and to see if you're still at risk.

I went into hospital in the early hours of the 23rd and came out on Christmas Day. Even though I had the all-clear from the hospital, my brain still felt incredibly sluggish, almost like a really bad hangover. I was struggling to make a cup of coffee so I definitely didn't feel like talking to a therapist for an hour as soon as I got home.

But I didn't have much choice. The community psychiatric nurse (CPN) sat across from me and Chris. I felt incredibly awkward. It was bad enough that I had to talk about why I had done it but I was sat next to Chris who I was emotionally disconnected from. The whole time I just wanted the world to open up and swallow me, but Chris and my friends said that I needed to do this to get well.

I didn't feel unwell. I had just had enough. But nobody seemed to understand that.

The CPN asked me some tough questions. Why did I feel it was the only way out? Why didn't I reach out to anyone? Why did I wait until I was alone? I would talk a little then Chris would interrupt, saying "I was the one that found him" and "didn't I care how it would affect him?"

I'm sure he was only trying to make me see sense but I felt like yelling at him. I couldn't, of course. I had nowhere else to live and who was going to take me in? I was a liability. I was stuck in this piss-poor life in a rubbish situation.

The CPN said that he had read my medical report and that I had definitely had a good go. He looked over at me and ask me if this is what I really wanted or was it a cry for help? In my head, I thought *are you seriously asking me that?* He asked if I knew how many pills I had taken. "Clearly not enough," I replied.

He then began to read off the list of how many empty blister packs Chris had found in the kitchen. Plus, a litre of gin and a bottle of champagne. My toxicity report showed my kidneys were suffering and that my creatinine levels were way above the normal range. He was shocked that I had survived.

The Christmas and New Year period was unbearable. I saw somebody for the next 10 days and, on their last visit, the CPN said, "We've been talking about you in the office. We're all surprised that you've made it this far without having drug and alcohol dependency and that this is your first suicide attempt, after the years of sexual abuse you went through."

I wish she had kept that to herself. After that visit, I was left to my own devices to get back to life, as if the past fortnight had never happened. Chris said that if I ever tried anything like that again, I'd be out. I could completely see where he was coming from; he never knew what he would be coming home to and that's not fair. I promised I wouldn't do it again.

When you're in that state of mind, you're not thinking about anyone else, let alone considering their thoughts and feelings. You are not thinking about the poor person that'll find you and the impact it'll have on their life. Friends told me that suicide was an easy way out and that it's selfish. I didn't disagree but, unless you've personally been in that state where you feel totally alone, worthless and that life is pointless, there is no way anyone would be able to comprehend just how dark your thoughts are. Passing hurt and anger onto you isn't right either; it's a horrible situation for everyone.

If you or someone you know is feeling suicidal, try and lift their mood with these ideas:

1. Be kind to yourself and eat good, natural whole foods – not junk food.

2. Find a warm and cosy place, close the curtains and listen to some guided meditation. This can help to calm your mind. Maybe use essential oils: camomile, lavender and eucalyptus is a super-relaxing combination.

3. Call someone rather than messaging them. Social interaction will help you to feel less alone.

4. Get out in the fresh air, even if it's just for 5 minutes. A little light helps to regulate mood even on a rainy day and try and connect to the things you see and hear.

5. Declutter an area that you spend a lot of time in. Doing something positive will make you feel in control and put you in a happier place.

6. Sing – even if you can't hold a note, play a song that you love and that makes you sing along. Grab a hairbrush or a spoon and dance along if you can. This will release endorphins and make you feel better.

Look for the hidden gifts that you already have in your life:

1. You have the freedom to love and to change your mindset

2. You have a roof over your head

3. Food in your fridge

4. You always have hope

Try reaching out for more support:

www.thehelphub.co.uk

www.thecalmzone.net

www.mind.org.uk

Living life Service; open from 1pm–9pm 0800 328 9655

www.samaritans.org or call 116 123.

Chapter 7

Losing Myself

'Finding my light in the most unexpected places'

Five months had now passed since those eventful few weeks and, from the outside, I was doing great at life. In fact, if I had been a movie star, But things at home were a living hell. Chris was avoiding all contact with me and, even though Mary was trying to support me, she was still Chris's mum. It must have been a horrid position to be in. I had huge respect for her. I was constantly snapping at her while she was trying to help me. Just like Grace had done all those years ago.

I was self-medicating with alcohol at the weekends. It was the only way I was managing to get through the weeks. This time, my poison was wine; I'd easily be downing 2 or 3 bottles on a Saturday evening after work. Then I'd spend all day at the gym on Sunday to burn off the booze, ready for work on Monday.

Unknown to me, I'd been getting complaints about the quality of my work and, as much as my clients loved me, they just couldn't cope with paying for bad hair. My work was the only thing I loved and, no matter what was going on in my life, I still looked forward to work. My boss had asked me to join her in the office for a chat.

"Lee, I don't know what's going on but I've had complaint after complaint about you. You're making stupid mistakes. And a few times you've come in and people have said that they could smell alcohol on your breath."

I was mortified. My beautiful ladies had to have bad hair because I couldn't hold my life together. They felt that they couldn't tell me directly. Who could blame them? I was a total mess.

My boss went on to say, "I love you, Lee, but after everything that happened around Christmas and now this, I'm sorry but I'm going to have to let you go. You need professional help."

Could my life get any worse? I now had to go home and tell Chris what a huge disappointment I was, not just to myself but to everyone that had stood by me as I tried to get on with life. How was I going to pay my way?

Chris took it well. I think he had been expecting it. Now that I was home constantly, I couldn't afford petrol or gym membership so, every now and again, Chris would fill up my tank and I could drive to see Sara. I think it was just so he could have some much-needed space.

Sara had a lovely summer house that was fully kitted out and she let me stay a few days. While I was there, I'd help with the house or I'd go and sit with her while she was at work. Sara and her husband are the kindest, most caring people you'd ever wish to meet. They would do anything for anyone and not expect anything in return. I felt so much love for her and her family.

Back at home, I had registered for benefits. It took weeks for them to come through. I was getting £533 a month: my rent and bills were £450, plus my phone bill and my car which left roughly £8 a week for food. Chris would help me out as much as he could and I'd pay him back the following month.

Every now and again, Chris would buy me a bottle of wine. He bought the nice stuff; I was buying the stuff at £3 a bottle. It was rancid but was better than nothing. Most days, I was out of it as my doctor had changed my morphine from tablets to transdermal patches because the risk of overdosing was lower.

Subconsciously, I had begun to look for a way out. Moving out wasn't an option: I had nowhere to go and I had no money. I had missed 4 phone bill payments and they had cut me off so the only time I could use my phone was while I was at home connected to Wi-Fi. I hardly went outside. It was a real crap situation and I was fast approaching a breakdown, which was hardly surprising given how the year had started.

Mary suggested that I see my doctor and tell them how I was feeling. She even offered to come with me, so I booked an appointment and she drove us down. Sat in the doctors waiting room, I started to cry. I felt desperate for help.

The doctor said that there was nothing that could be done medically for me and they referred me to the CPN that worked in the practice. The CPN was a lovely lady but she was no help as she could only suggest techniques that may help me to cope, things like going to the gym. I'd been doing them all for months and, even though I couldn't use the gym anymore, I had been going on daily walks with Mary. I was doing everything I could at home but nothing was helping. The CPN said she would speak to the doctor about trying me on different anti-depressants but the doctor was unwilling to try me on anything new.

This went on for weeks. I was just passed to and from the doctor to the CPN and back again. I was reading self-help books on how to get over depression and completing online courses. I had even tried to go to a men's support group, which was a no go: as soon as a guy raised his voice unexpectedly, my PTSD would fire-up and my fears from my childhood came flooding back. I went once and never went back. It was supposed to be helping with anxiety, not making it 10 times as worse!

Anyone that's been in the 'system' will know that dealing with mental health or distress is a horrible place to be as everyone is stuck too. Your friends and family don't know what to do to help you and they're not professionally trained to deal with the issues that you're having. Your GP is a 'general' doctor who doesn't necessarily have any special training in mental health. Unless they have an interest in it themselves, they're often stuck to know what to do. A CPN is a qualified nurse who has had some specialist training in mental health. There are self-referral mental health services which offer group or one-to-one therapies and these can take anywhere from 5 weeks to 3 months to access if you meet their criteria. I was going to my doctor and CPN weekly, begging for their help as I was having thoughts of wanting to take my life again. But neither could offer me a solution. I felt like I was an inconvenience to my doctor. The CPN told me that she really did feel for me but there was only so much that she could do.

I was at the point of not sleeping. I would be awake constantly for days and then sleep for a week. At times, I didn't eat from one week to the next. I had just given up. I felt totally disconnected from the world and everyone in it.

***

An old client had been in touch and she needed her hair styled for a family wedding. She wanted to know if I'd be willing to do it, but she couldn't afford to pay me and so asked if I'd do it for 4 bottles of wine and a takeaway as she could use her credit card for that. I jumped at the chance. I'd not had a 'proper' drink in months and it was great seeing her and we had a really great night. At the end of it, she got me an Uber home. Chris was out again so I opened the 3rd bottle of wine. Alcohol and morphine isn't the best combination, especially when you're emotionally and financially broken. But I didn't have anything else to do and I sat on the floor looking out of the balcony, looking up at the grey sky and thinking what's the point? What kind of life is this? I have no purpose other than sitting in a house day in and day out. I started to think about all the things I didn't have.

Back in December, my friends were annoyed that I hadn't written any goodbye letters, I was just going to go and leave them wondering why. This time, I thought I'd send out text messages in the early hours, making sure they'd be asleep and wouldn't see anything until the morning. Chris was away and, this time I had made a plan to make sure no one would find me.

Because my doctor wouldn't give me any sleeping pills, I had been getting them from a friend. They no longer had an effect on her and she knew I was struggling to sleep so she thought was helping me out. But unknown to her, I had been saving them up. Plus, I'd been saving most of the morphine patches. I had stuck all of the patches on my arms and chest while writing these messages. I had less than 6 friends, so it didn't take me long and, about an hour before I sent them, I started my 4th bottle of wine. I was starting to feel the effects of the patches. I had gotten dressed and was planning on walking over to the fields near the house; I'd already picked out a spot to sit and wait for Mum.

I knew the sleeping pills would take at least 30 minutes to get into my system.

I had everything ready to go. In my drunken confusion, I had sent the messages out around 3am and, by chance, one friend, Sandra, had seen my text. She immediately rang to see what was happening and, at this point, I had peeled the patches off and had begun to chew them. I can't remember much after that point, I must have passed out.

Three days later, I woke up in hospital again. But this time I was on a high dependency unit with a heart tracer attached to my chest and drips attached. I had a catheter to drain my bladder and a nurse sat in my room because I was at high risk of crashing. Just like before, the crisis team came to visit me on the unit to see if I wanted their help again. I agreed; I needed help.

My friend Sandra had sent me a text, explaining that she needed some space. I didn't know at the time but she had driven over to check on me thinking I had sent her a drunken text. In fact, she had found me unconscious and if it hadn't been for her partner, I wouldn't be alive. They gave me CPR. It was just too traumatic for them but she wanted me to know that if I was ever in that situation again I'd get help.

I felt devastated and ashamed that I had put them in that position and, as much as I wanted to erase the distress I had caused, there wasn't anything I could do. They were both great friends and I had ruined our friendship forever.

This time, when the crisis team came for their daily visits to my home, Chris wasn't around, which helped immensely. I could open up about and my thoughts and feelings for the first time and I knew that I wouldn't be judged. I saw a CPN every day for 3 weeks and then they referred me to home and community mental health services, which gave me access to ongoing treatment. This included trying new anti-depressants and talking therapy. At this point, Chris and Mary wanted them to section me. This massively broke me. They knew about my dad and I was nothing like that.

I needed real support, rather than people sugar-coating everything. I spoke to the psychiatrist looking after my case and she reassured me that they wouldn't be sectioning me and that it wasn't even an option. This reassured me slightly but the thought of it terrified me. I remember what the ward was like when my dad was held there.

A mental health unit is nothing like a medical ward. Instead of patients sharing a ward that's for a particular physical health condition, with a mental health ward different conditions are all mixed in together: from severe depression to schizophrenia. One minute, everything would be calm and quiet, the next all hell would break loose. Alarms sounding, panic lights flashing, patients and staff running around, staff talking over transceivers trying to calm situations down. It was a scary place and, to an outsider, seemed like there wasn't any order.

I asked the psychiatrist if mental health conditions are hereditary. I was terrified at the thought of turning into my dad. Again, she reassured me that I had nothing to worry about. There isn't any evidence to suggest that it is.

Clearly, my situation was bad. My friends had started to distance themselves too. Sara could no longer cope and she had her own family and issues to deal with. I totally understood that she needed to focus on herself but it didn't make it any less painful. I cried for days after this as she meant everything to me. But I loved her enough to respect her wishes, so I stepped away.

***

A month had now past and I was starting to find my feet again. A combination of therapy and weekly counselling along with the change in my medication were helping. Even my GP seemed to be more interested in helping me get better. I was going for long walks daily, which helped to lift my mood, and I was doing a couple of free online courses to help me rewire my brain into more positive thinking patterns. All things considered, I was doing well, which is probably why Chris thought it was a good time to talk to me about moving out.

He just couldn't cope with having me around anymore. Besides, he had just started seeing someone and me being at home made it awkward. Chris gave me 3 months to find somewhere, which quickly turned into 5. I had to register at the council for a flat, but the housing list was endless. They had no idea when something suitable would become available. I had no savings to just move out and privately rent. The odd friend I did have I didn't know well enough to ask if I could stay at theirs.

Chris was talking about my situation to one of his friends and it just so happened that her mum was living in a 2-bed house and she was struggling to pay the bills. I hardly knew this lady – I had only met her once a few years ago – but I knew from Chris that she, too, had major depression issues. I was, therefore, reluctant to move into her home. But what other option did I have?

I arranged to talk to her and look at her spare room. She lived on a quiet street and her home was clean but extremely cluttered. She didn't want a bond, she wanted the first month's rent up front, which I didn't have as I had just paid Chris. I rang him and explained the situation. He really needed me out so offered to lend me the money and I could pay him back when I could afford to. I had applied for PIP (personal independence payment, a specialised benefit given to people with long term ill-health or disabilities. This is hard to get and it's a very drawn out process that can last for 2 years before a decision is made) so hopefully it wouldn't be long before I could pay him back for everything I had borrowed.

For me to feel relaxed in a space it needs to be free of clutter, neat and tidy. But Debbie quite the opposite. She was a hoarder to the extent that you wouldn't know where to sit because even the couches were cluttered with blankets and cushions. If you had been sat on the couch then, as soon as you stood, she'd move in quickly to replace the cushions! She had an enormous collection of decorative trinkets and plaques with inspirational quotes, "home is where the heart is" or "queen of cleaning" hanging off the walls, doors and any corners that she could find. But it was her home and I respected how she lived. I thought I'd only be using the kitchen to cook then I'll be in my room, so it wouldn't bother me that much.

I moved in that weekend.

I could only take the things that I could fit into my car, which wasn't so bad seeing as I was moving into an already cluttered spare room. Thankfully, Debbie had cleared out a few draws for me and within days of me being there, I could tell it wasn't going to be easy. She had a lot of issues herself; it was very much a case of out of the frying pan and into the fire. But it was my actions that had gotten me into this and, for the time being, there were no other options.

Some mornings, I would hear Debbie walking around the house shouting at herself. "You're so fucking fat nobody will ever want you," or "move, you fucking lazy bastard."

At first, I thought she was talking to me. But after talking to her brother I found out it's just how she was. I still thought it was unnerving and it put me on edge. Whenever she wasn't at work, she would drink a lot and smoke like a chimney. At first, I'd join her for a drink. But it was a trigger for me to feeling bad and having negative thoughts so, after a while, I just used to sit in my room and keep out of the way.

For the times I couldn't avoid her and needed to use the kitchen, it was a difficult experience. She had a special pan for everything, God help me if I had used a pan that was for boiling eggs but I had used it to boil pasta! She would never say anything to me directly; instead, she would walk around the house muttering under her breath. I couldn't see the problem and I washed everything immediately after I used it.

I knew that, deep down, Debbie was a good person. I just tried to keep my head down and remind myself that all this was my only choice. I kept out of her way.

With the stress, I had started to get flare-ups and my doctor had started me on a course of steroids to get on top of it. But things became too unmanageable at home and I needed a stay in hospital for a few days. I started to look for something else but every time I found something, it would be quickly taken or wasn't suitable for one reason or another. I remember thinking that the right place will become available when the time is right.

Home from hospital, I walked in to find Debbie waiting for me. "Lee, this isn't working for me. I need my own space. I've lived on my own for far too long and I just feel overcrowded with you being here." Part of me felt relieved. I had felt on edge since moving in that it would be a relief to get away. "I'll give you 2 weeks to find something."

Holy shit! "Two weeks? Are you kidding Debbie? I've just got out of hospital and I've just paid you for another month."

I didn't know what to do so I rang Chris. "I'm so sorry that I need to ask you this but would you possibly mind if …" and before I could finish, he said no. It just wouldn't work, he said. And he was away on holiday the next day and didn't want the stress.

It was the next evening when Debbie piled on more pressure. She came back from work and said, "I know I said 2 weeks Lee, but I need you to go now. I've been thinking about it all day and you treat my spare room like it's your own. There are clothes everywhere and you always leave your toiletries in the bathroom. I'm sick of telling you that you need to keep everything in your room and in your drawers so I don't have to look at them. I don't want to feel like I'm sharing my house."

I went into panic mode. I asked Debbie for part of the rent back and set about packing up. I rang Mary to ask if I could sleep on her couch for a week or so until something came up. I explained the situation I was in and Mary replied with an absolute no. She apologised and put the phone down.

I rang an old friend, Alice. I knew she didn't have much room – she was massively into crafts and had stuff everywhere – but I thought it was still worth a try. I spoke to her and, even though she empathised, she couldn't help.

Alice had recommended that I call the emergency shelter. She said they could give me advice on what I needed to do as I now had nowhere to live. Even though it's called 'emergency shelter' it wasn't something that they could help me with immediately. They told me that I needed to register as homeless and then I could try for the emergency shelter, which meant that I would be given a time to attend. It was first come, first served and if I wasn't lucky enough to get a place, I would need to sleep on the street or in my car. As the man on the phone explained everything to me, I had an overwhelming feeling of dread in the pit of my stomach.

The car was packed; it was time to leave.

Debbie told me that her daughter's friend had to sleep in hostels with her kids. "They're not as bad as you think and they won't see you on the streets because you've got Crohn's." The next sentence baffled me. "Will you keep in touch and let me know what's happening?" she said. "Anyway, I best get going, my bath's nearly ran."

I literally couldn't speak. I just got into my car and drove to a nearby supermarket car park. I tried to calm myself down and try to think rationally. It was close to midnight by now and it was bitterly cold and a cloudless sky. I got out of the car and stood, looking up at the stars.

I yelled up at the sky. "Please! Bring into my life a home that's safe and warm. A family of my own – and a dog. I need these *now*!"

This was something from a book that I had read years ago but I had ever been at the stage of desperation that I was now. I envisioned what a home would feel like, what would it smell like, furniture, a family and what that would all look like … I put every ounce of my being into the image and attached strong emotions to it.

If anyone had seen or heard me, they must have thought I was a right plonker!

I got back into my car and kept staring up at the universe until my eyes stung. I was staring with intent; I didn't want to miss a sign.

I must have been there for an hour. A police car drove onto the car park and I didn't know if someone had called them or it was just coincidence. Either way, I didn't fancy needing to explain myself so I drove back round to Debbie's estate. I thought that if they followed me, at least I could knock on her door to say I had forgotten something. But they didn't.

I was still thinking about my order to the universe when Grace popped into my head. Could I call her? I'd not seen her in 13 years. Would she even have the same landline number? And even if I did call her, would she even want to hear from me? I thought about her and the kids and started to sob.

I thought about a small story I had read somewhere and it opened my mind a little wider, it read:

A dam to a river had burst in a small village and flooded homes. A man climbed up onto the roof of his house where he sat and prayed. "Dear God, please save me. I need your help!"

As he sat waiting for God to save him, a neighbour was sat with his family on their roof and shouted to the man, "We have a rope. We can help you onto our roof. We have shelter and food."

The man shouted "No, thank you. My God will save me!"

A boat came by and shouted to the man, "Get in the boat, we'll save you."

"No," said the man, "my God will save me."

Some time had passed by and the weather was getting worse.

A helicopter came over and shouted down, "We'll lower the ladders and take you to safety."

"No thank you," said the man, "I'm waiting for my God. He will save me."

A hurricane came and swept the man off the roof to his death.

When the man arrived in heaven he said to God, "I prayed for you to save me and you never came."

126

God replied, "I sent you a neighbour, a boat and a helicopter."

Did Grace pop into my head by pure chance or because this was a sign from the universe? I took a chance. I called the number that Grace had 13 years ago. It began to ring and I immediately wondered what to do if she didn't live there anymore. A man answered. "Hi, it's Lee. Grace's brother." He sounded surprised. "Is Grace there?"

I heard him pass the phone to my sister and I got straight to the point.

"Grace, I need help and I'm sorry that I'm calling you after so long. You're my last chance before I need to register as homeless." I filled her in on the details and asked if she could help me

She said, "I'll need to discuss it with Paul and the kids first, Lee. We've not seen you for 13 years, a lot has happened."

I totally understood. "If you can't, it's okay. And I'll be okay. I will sort something. Honestly, I'll be fine." She asked where I was and I replied, "I'm in my car. I don't have anywhere to go." Grace suggested booking into a hotel for the night, and we'd be able to discuss things in the morning. It hadn't even crossed my mind.

I booked a cheap hotel for the night and drove over. Once there, I checked in and asked the receptionist if my car would be safe as it had the entire contents of my life in it. She looked at me with a puzzled look on her face. I said quickly, "Oh, I've fallen out with my boyfriend *again*," and I laughed. "I'll give it a couple of days to calm down, then I'll move back in." She started to laugh and replied and told me her brother and his partner were like that too.

There was no way I was going to tell her the real reason why my life was squeezed into my car but, at the same time, I felt like I needed to explain myself. Those years of being a stylist came to good use and I was able to think on the spot!

"If I was you," she said, "I'd bring everything into the hotel. I wouldn't risk it." One of the guys that worked in the kitchen helped me to bring everything in; I bought him a beer to say thanks.

I didn't sleep at all. I kept going out to check that my car was still safe in between looking up information on the internet about what registering to become homeless entailed and what I'd do if I didn't meet the requirements for emergency housing. How long could I be on the streets? The estimate was 8 weeks before you would qualify for housing. I needed to prepare myself in case Grace couldn't help.

I prayed to the universe for 8 hours straight. At no time did I let the other options enter my mind or thoughts. I had done my research on my plan B and I left that where it was. There wasn't anything I could do at 2am.

I just gave my entire heart, soul and being over to the universe. I repeated my order constantly, making the images in my mind bigger, brighter and full of colour. I imagined what Grace and Paul now looked like, and the same for my niece and nephew. I didn't leave anything to chance, even down to what I thought they would be wearing.

Even down to the smell of Grace's home.

The next morning, Grace rang and said that she had spoken to Paul and the kids. She said that they all agreed they couldn't see me homeless. "Why don't you get yourself together and drive over later. I'll be home from work this afternoon so there's no rush." I thanked her for saving me.

On the drive down I got thinking about why we had fallen out all those years ago.

Twelve years ago, I received a call from the sexual health clinic to tell me that I had been in contact with someone that had tested positive for a sexually transmitted infection and the clinic advised me to go in for a full screening. I hadn't long been out of a long term relationship and had been seeing a guy for a few months. I had been tested just before seeing this guy and was all clear so I gave him a call to ask if he knew anything about it. I didn't get a chance to talk to him: he had blocked me. I couldn't call, text or even contact him on Facebook. "What a wanker," I thought. But I was grateful that he had the decency to give them my number and at least I knew I needed a test.

I went along to the clinic and got tested. Thankfully, it came back negative but they recommended that I go back in 10 weeks for a retest. Only a few weeks away from my test being due, I had been admitted by my GP with chronic diarrhoea and bowel pain. This was before I had the diagnosis of IBS. My STI test was back and I tested positive for HIV.

As a precaution, I had been reading up on the latest research in treatment and had learnt as much as I could just in case. I was referred to an infectious disease specialist because I had the complication of my bowel and autoimmune system and, on my first appointment, I asked to be started on antiretrovirals immediately. My doctor said that they don't normally start someone with such a high CD4 count (the higher the count, the stronger the immune system is) but I insisted that it's my health and so my choice. I wanted it to become undetectable so that I could eliminate the possibility of passing it onto a future partner.

I was started on the medication 2 weeks later!

This was a huge deal for me at the time and I needed to talk to someone I could trust and that wouldn't judge me. I confided in Grace. She didn't judge me and she just took it in her stride. But she also needed to talk to someone and so she told her best friend. At the time, I didn't see that she also needed to talk to someone and, unfortunately, I reacted in a very inconsiderate way. I felt like she had betrayed my trust at a time when I was newly diagnosed. I felt ashamed and dirty and the thought of someone else knowing. I just couldn't cope so I fell out with Grace and took her out of my life.

Now, after all those years had passed, I hoped that all our emotions had passed too. I had paid the ultimate price for reacting like I had and I had lost out on seeing my beautiful niece and nephew growing up. I couldn't get those years back. The fact that she welcomed me into her home with arms wide open was all their reassurance I needed.

I had zero doubt that it was down to the universe that I now had a home that was safe and warm, as well as a family. They even had a dog! Even the front door was exactly as I had imagined it to be – and there was no way I could have known.

Grace helped me to unload the car into her kitchen and that's when I started to cry. Everything I owned was in a black bin-liner. All I had to show for my 38 years on this earth.

Grace gave me a hug. "Everything will work out. Do you want a cuppa?" I had forgotten what she sounded like. She sounded just like Mum and, because she had lived in the same town the whole of her life, her accent hadn't changed one bit. Whereas I had lived in 4 cities since I had left home, so my accent had been watered down quite a bit.

Grace hadn't changed, apart from her gorgeous brunette locks that were now an ash blonde. But I guess it is easier to hide the greys! Apart from that, she still looked incredible. She had always worked out and was clearly still doing so. Paul looked the same as I had remembered but now with a little less hair. But I could hardly say anything: mine had completely gone!

I was so nervous to see the kids. When I left, my nephew was 12 and was now was fast approaching 25. The first thing that struck me was his height. A face full of stubble – even now I'm used to the stubble I still think it's crazy. He had grown up to be an amazing young man who has travelled and is well-educated. He's working full-time and has his own business. My niece was 8 and she's now 21. She is unbelievably beautiful, both inside and out. She still looks the same, just taller. She's a nurse. Both are extremely polite and well-spoken and are living their lives with direction. I know my mum would have been so proud of them all.

Is my relationship with my sister perfect? No. But I *have* a relationship with her. And I now know my niece and nephew. I'm in a position that we can grow together rather than apart.

A part of me wished that I had a smidge of what Grace has: stability, a real family of her own and unconditional love until death and beyond for somebody else. I used to struggle to love myself.

If, like me, you have struggled or are struggling to see how amazing you really are and need to love yourself again, I have created a fast and easy skill for you to work through to rediscover how incredible you really are. It has – and still does – work for me and many of my clients. The science behind it has been heavily documented so I know, almost for certain, that it will work for you too!

I do know that, without any doubt, you are brilliant. I am giving you my light and love so that you have the power to find your own.

Chapter 8

Who Am I?

The 'Who Am I?' skill

When you are struggling to see how amazing you are, this skill will help you to see just how incredible you are and that you are here for a worthwhile purpose.

These simple steps will help you to regain your ability to see how much you are loved and respected. It will help you to identify all your positives and reveal any negatives that you are carrying with you.

Both are gifts …

Positive feedback will give you an immediate sense of self-love, knowing how much you are loved by others too.

Negative feedback isn't really all negative. In fact, it is the complete opposite! It allows us to see how we can correct something that we weren't aware of and become even greater.

You are going to send a message to a friend or someone that loves and respects you, and someone whose opinion you trust. Only ask the people who you know won't lie or sugar-coat the truth. This way, you will believe what they say – even if you don't believe it *yet*.

Part 1

Start by sending:

I know that you are busy but when you have some time spare, I really would appreciate your help if you would answer these questions about me.

> How do you see me? or Who is *insert your name here.*
>
> Why should someone trust me?
>
> What makes me different from your other friends or loved ones?

Then finish with:

Please be kind and honest. I love and respect you. Thank you for your help!

Brace yourself. Sometimes the result will surprise you!

Write down all the positives. You'll need these for part 2 when we reprogram your mind, helping you to realise you are a great person.

Write down all the negatives too. Are they really a negative? Don't look at these in a bad light; nobody is perfect so you're not alone! Negatives are positives in disguise. Now that we know what they are, it means that we can work on them to become your strengths.

Here are some examples of what I got from my friends when I sent them the same messages.

Jodie wrote:

Who am I? Lee, you are loyal, kind and extremely trustworthy.

Why trust me? You always speak your mind when I ask you to and you tell me the truth without offending or needing to be harsh to get the message across. You never gossip or talk about other people's problems and I know I can tell you anything and you won't judge.

Why am I different? You never pretend to be something that you're not. My other friends fall into categories but with you, I can talk about anything and everything from my skincare to my child's poos! There's never judgement, you just take everything in your stride.

Negatives? The only thing I would change is that I would love to speak on the phone more rather than always messaging.

Now, I'll break this down into easy to read statements:

1. I am always honest and true to myself and others. I am authentic.

2. I care about people's feelings and I never judge. I am trustworthy and kind.

3. I will call my friend and put valuable time into our friendship. I am supportive and I value others.

Scott wrote:

Who am I? Lee is kind, caring and always sees others as unique.

Why trust me? You always go out your way for others, no matter what your own circumstances you are.

Why am I different? You view others as individuals first and take people as you find them. You accept them for their true selves, no matter what that is, unlike so many others that see a person's situation before they see the person. You believe the reasons for doing something are more important than just going through the motions to reach an end goal.

Negatives? You get easily distracted with big goals.

Broken down to:

1. I am respectful of others and see a person's inner self rather than their shells. I am respectful.

2. I never want to feel that someone needs to put on a front. I am accepting of everyone.

3. I need to break down big goals into micro goals rather than taking leaps to make any goal easily achievable.

I am possible – anything is possible.

Try and turn your positive statements into one, short statement. This may take some practice but you'll get there, it just takes a little time.

Now to rewire your mind.

Don't worry – it's not painful and it is super-easy to do!

It has been proven by science and has been extensively documented by many people in the field of mind development. The only problem is not many make it easy to understand how to use this method to get results fast.

I know that your time is precious and that's why I have developed the 'How to' so that you can get everything you want and need in as little time as possible.

You'll need to spend around an hour on part 1 to figure out your 'I am' statements but after that, part 2 will take you only 10 minutes. You can use the remaining 1,430 minutes (that's 23 hours and 50 minutes!) in your day and totally forget about your 'I am' statements and allow your mind to sort out the rest.

"All that we are is the result of what we have thought." [Buddha]

Here's the science.

This is all down to your RAS (reticular activating system). The RAS controls our sleep patterns and our consciousness; its job is to filter all the information we take in daily and to organise and prioritise it. It does this by creating new neuron pathways so that our brains can access information quickly. A good example of this is our 'autopilot mode'. Have you ever driven to work and can't remember how you got there? Or you've cooked your family's favourite meal and, when you serve it up, can't remember the process? Well, that's your RAS at work.

Our brains are hardwired to love routine. Our brains make a log of anything that we do or think about regularly so that it can access that information fast the next time we need it. If we can focus on positive messages, our brains will look out for more positive messages.

141

Unfortunately, the same goes for negatives. Just like when you focus on finding a red car you'll notice just how many red cars there are. The same goes for when you like a baby's name and, suddenly, you notice it everywhere! Before you focused on that name; you can't remember hearing it at all.

Simply by focusing on your 'I am' statements at bedtime, you will be hardwiring your mind and, before you know it, you will step into your magnificence!

This is a reason why meditation is so powerful. It allows you to cut out all distractions and slows your mind, meaning that the positives you think of become who you are and what you are. But meditation isn't for everyone. It has taken me years to love and look forward to my 'power hour', which I do just before sleep. I started with just 10 minutes before going to bed. Once you're in the habit of writing down your 'I ams', they'll become second nature and you won't need to write them down. At the start, we need to focus our minds and this is done by the physical act of writing.

Once you start to see tangible results from your 'I ams', it will give you the positive confirmations you so rightly deserve. See, I told you it was easy!

The next skill will help you attract the material things into your life and, as you've just done, it's easy. You've got this!

Whether you are wanting to attract good health, money or even a new car, the process is the same. It still involves your RAS but on a much deeper level this time. You will need more practice but the process isn't any harder to grasp.

We all have and use both the right and left sides of our brains but some people are better at using one or the other. Imagine what you could achieve if you could use both as well as each other.

We can use the images in our mind to attract what we want into our life, just like a magnet attracts metal.

I will show you how to use your imagination and creativity to ignite your RAS to bring anything that you want into your life. Just like walking and eating are second nature soon this will be too! As a baby, you were guided through walking and eating. Through that repetition, you now are an expert in these things. The same goes for anything that used to be impossible until you learnt how to do it and now it's easy!

All you need is a belief that you can and action to make it so and it will be.

"

Part 2

How to put in an order to the universe.

Choose one thing that you want to focus on.

1. Put on a piece of music that allows you to completely focus on your thoughts and that will help you to distance yourself from outside distractions. I use a 417 Hz frequency, you can find videos on YouTube for free and you want a running time of 30–60 minutes.

But do whatever helps *you* to focus. Don't worry if you can only manage a few minutes at a time, just remember that when a child starts to walk for the first time, they only manage a few steps. The more you practise, the stronger you'll become and, naturally, you'll be able to put more and more time into it.

2. Lie or sit, whichever is the most comfortable for you – eyes open or closed.

3. Focus your attention on your breathing – take a few slow deep breaths and let any tension go.

4. Think of yourself feeling strong and remember all the good things your friends said about you.

5. Now think about the thing that you want to bring into your life. Make that image bright and full of colour; make it full of detail. What does it feel like?

6. Imagine you already have that thing in your life. Give yourself a sense of the pleasure it brings you. How amazing does it make you feel? See yourself celebrating with your loved ones and hear them congratulating you and telling you how incredible you are!

7. See yourself really enjoying your life. Allow yourself to experience how good this feels!

8. Amplify your emotions as if you've just stepped into your new life. Embrace all the incredible sensations that you are now experiencing!

Now let it all go. Let everything melt away into your unconsciousness.

Your RAS or the universe (either is right, as long as you believe that's the important thing) will do all the work to bring these things into your life. The more relaxed and the more emotions you connect to your images, the faster they'll appear in your life.

Do this once a day. A great time to find the time is when you first wake up before you even get out of bed. Try setting your alarm 20 minutes earlier than you need to. It won't take long before you're naturally waking up, as your mind wants to feel amazing. After a few weeks, you'll look forward to doing this visualisation skill every morning.

It won't be long until you can do a full hour or whatever is right for you.

Once you've completed your visualisation, completely forget about it and get on with your day. Trust that your RAS, the universe or your higher power will make all this possible. If you struggle to see yourself living the life that you want, think of somebody else that once had your limitations and has succeeded!

This works but you need to trust in the process.

Remember, your RAS thrives on routine. The more intensely you can connect all your senses to the images in your mind, the faster the RAS will lay down the new neurons to attract everything you want into your life.

Remember, *be kind to yourself*. Don't forget to reward yourself. In the beginning, I used to reward myself with a pamper night, like a new skin cream or a new piece of clothing. As long as your reward makes you feel good and has a positive impact on you, *go for it*! After a while, I didn't need a reward. I just loved being absorbed in creating the things that I wanted.

Chapter 9

Total Freedom

'Letting go of everything that has held me back'

B ack when I was 8 years old, I had started a lifelong addiction to sugar and fat-filled foods, better known as 'junk food'. It was going to stay with me until I took my power back aged 40. *Thirty-two years* of addiction had caused me to not socialise because I thought others would be judging me on my size. There was always a strong feeling of dread when I needed a new outfit, either for a special occasion or just because I had outgrown my regular clothes. And even when I had lost weight and felt amazing, the beast in the back of my mind would pipe up with "don't eat that, don't drink that, you'll put all that weight back on …"

My mind would torment me. *What's wrong with me? Why can't I stick to a diet? I'm weak and don't have any willpower. I don't have an off switch; I just keep going until it's all gone. Everyone else sticks to a diet, so why can't I? I look horrendous. Nobody is going to want me. I'm so fat.*

I was always thinking about my next 'fix'. Even while having breakfast, I was already thinking about lunch. Then, for the rest of the day. I would be thinking of what I can have next with a cup of tea? Maybe pork scratchings or my favourite chocolate bar, A sodding apple isn't a treat – I want something naughty!

If I managed to get through the day, by drinking my body weight in herbal tea and water, the beast would wake up later at dinner time. "I've been looking forward to this all day," I would think. Then after, when I was stuffed, I'd then fancy something sweet.

This cycle of torment and torture would go on for weeks and months at a time. I could stop myself from eating if I threw the treats in the bin. But then, on my desperate days, I'd find myself hours later rooting through the bin bag to retrieve something.

At Christmas, I'd buy cheeseboards, biscuits and chocolates for gifts. They'd be wrapped and ready to be given, only for me, a few days later, to open them and eat them. I'd be forced to buy other gifts, something inedible.

The craziest moments would be when was out food shopping or out for a coffee. I would feel like I was going out my mind and, if anyone could hear what was happening in my head, they would think I was crazy and needing to be sectioned …

The devil would tell me to have that treat. "Nobody will know. You deserve it. Go on, just have one." The angel was encouraging me to stay away, "You don't need it, you've been doing so well don't ruin it now, you're stronger than this."

So, what is addiction?

If you can't resist or it takes over your mind for most of your waking hours, it's fair to say you need help to break the control it has over you. When we think of addiction these probably come to mind:

Alcohol

Drugs

Sex

But food is a big addiction too but, because we need food to live, it's harder to do a 'detox' like you would for those above. Taking those away and working through issues psychologically to be free of the addiction is going to be easier than it will be for a food addiction, given that we need food to survive.

The issue isn't finding a diet that works for you. Anything that causes a calorie deficit will generally result in you losing weight. The real issue is your emotional connection to your food 'drug' of choice. In the past, I have had addictions to both cocaine and methamphetamine (crystal meth) and know what big doses of 'happy' hormone feel like. For me, it was far easier to get clean from the drugs than to free myself from the addiction to junk food.

I was able to overcome my addictions with the skill that I'll describe at the end of this chapter. I didn't have therapy or any other intervention. I simply used what I am going to teach you and you will become free of the need and free of the tortures of your addiction. You 100% can do this!

Why do we feel so powerless and hopeless when faced with addictions? Anything that fires up the limbic system within your brain and stimulates the dopamine receptors, the part of the brain that's responsible for motivation and reward, has the potential to cause an addiction. But how and why?

Here is some more of the science.

Whenever we consume sugar, we have a huge increase of dopamine the happy hormone which is nearly as much of a increase as what cocaine users get, Shocking, isn't it, and no wonder that we feel like we're going crazy when we're only having a little sugar. We feel like we desperately need more when trying to restrict our intake of that 'treat'. Just like any other addiction, we can't just have a little and be okay, we want *more*. Then, over a prolonged period of time, we will build a tolerance to that small amount and now need *even more* to get the same feeling.

Why does this happen?

Our brains are hardwired to respond to rewards. This was used to motivate us to act and search for food, back when we were hunter-gathers. The increase of dopamine made sure that our behaviours would be indispensable to the survival of the human race.

If food or sex didn't give us pleasure, we wouldn't be encouraged to eat or to procreate. The brain developed the dopamine response to make sure we carried on doing these things to make sure that we survived. Unfortunately, our brains haven't had time to adapt to our 'new' lifestyle where food is readily available and we can have sugar, fat, salt, drugs, sex and alcohol any time we want. We have become dopamine resistant, which is why we can't stop at just a little.

The reason that you have an uncontrollable need to unwrap gifts to get your 'fix' or you cannot leave those biscuits alone, hasn't got anything to do with you not having willpower. You are not weak, it's just that our brains are doing what they have evolved to do. We have connected with that item and it makes us feel good.

Here's a great example of how it works. Look at this image.

You probably picked out your favourite immediately. Your midbrain decides within 15 seconds which then sends a signal to your limbic system to give you a spike in dopamine. The reason for this is that pleasure, just from looking at your favourite, makes you want more.

You remember how rewarding that treat was and, because you've had a sense of that pleasure just from looking at your favourite, you already want more, which is why you reach These are some of the effects that excess dopamine in the brain can cause:

Weak-willed and impulsive behaviour

Need for instant gratification

Lack of motivation

Withdrawal from social situations

Paranoia

Suspicious personality

High levels of dopamine are also found in people with ADHD.

How many do you recognise in yourself? I got 6 out of the 7.

When I realised this, it totally shifted how I thought about myself. Everything I had thought about myself wasn't true: it's all down to how our brains are developed. Knowing this, the cure becomes super-easy. I needed a dopamine detox.

We end up chasing a dopamine hit to feel good and, most of the time, once we've had the 'treat', we often feel like it wasn't worth it. Our dopamine is just to compel us to get more dopamine. Our brains want

156

to feel good so once we've had that hit, the levels of dopamine decrease and that's why we feel it wasn't worth it. Dopamine controls our wants and desires but not if we enjoy something else instead.

How do we break free?

A dopamine detox

Dopamine creates a cycle within us that can be incredibly hard to break. We need to remove anything that gives pleasure. Instantly, this will reduce the amount that's released by our brains and thus breaking that negative habit!

The Dopamine Fast was developed by Dr Cameron Sepah, a psychologist who based his research on a behavioural therapy technique called 'stimulus control'. The detox won't increase or decrease the amount of dopamine you have in your body, but it will control your wants and desires, which will give you back a feeling of being in control. That beast will become an ant and you can say goodbye to temptation.

We need to remove your 'treat' from your life. Don't worry, you'll be able to enjoy a treat after this and you'll still be able to enjoy it. All you are doing is gaining control over it. You will be able to stop, think and make your own decisions. We are taking control of our midbrain so that now you'll become unstoppable!

1. Identify your temptation.

2. Let people know that you're stepping away from your 'treat' so that they don't unknowingly tempt you. Plus it will give you a sense of accountability and help to keep you on track.

3. Start your detox first thing in the morning. Get everything prepared the day before. Get whatever 'treat' it is out of the way, or as far away as possible. Out of sight, out of mind!

4. Maintain this for 24 hours. Wake up without temptation and go to sleep without it too.

When you feel you have more self-control, try doing this for a week. I did 24 hours and had a break. Then, a few days later, I did 3 days at a time building up to a whole week. Now, I no longer have that desire to go through the bin after the 'treat' I thrown away. If I want chocolate or wine, I think about it for 15–30 seconds then decide if I actually want it or not.

Remember *you* are amazing. Just by reading through this, the process will stick with you and be ready for you whenever you feel you need to break free.

Chapter 10

Conclusion And Action Steps

Writing *Break Free* was incredibly hard. It has forced me to revisit some of the hardest and most challenging times in my life and I had to constantly remind myself that the purpose of this book is to help others that have been through or are currently going through similar experiences. I can show how to truly break free from the cycle of suffering. To do that, I needed to lay everything out on the table.

The freedom I have today is the result of putting into practice the skills in this book. They may have needed repeating until they became part of who I am but I realise now that the things I went through were training me for a greater purpose. That purpose is to help others through their own dark times. I had to remain transparent and honest to write my story so that my readers knew that they weren't alone. I had to keep revisiting the 'Who am I?' skill to know that I was strong enough and honest enough to get me through this. I used to drive myself into a deep dark hole with the conversations I had in my own head that kept me from being free of my own emotions and that kept me in that hole for longer, letting my hope and purpose slip away.

Writing the most painful, embarrassing and gut-wrenching moments of my life was hard, never mind publishing them for complete strangers to read. But every time I slipped off course, something would gently guide me back. Either a conversation with a friend about their suffering or a reference in a movie that would seem bright and bold, as if it was just for me. I couldn't keep others in pain when I could have the solution to end their suffering.

Take a deeper look into your own experiences and try the skills again. With these pointers in mind, you may discover something new.

Disassociation

1.   Find your pebble.

2.   Take charge. When you may have thought that reconnecting just happened by chance, now you can direct yourself out from being disconnected.

3.   Trust in the process.

4.   Have patience. It will become easier and you just need to practice.

Forgiveness

1.   See yourself how others see you.

2.   Treat yourself with love and kindness.

3.   Borrow faith from the ones that love and care for you.

4.   Stop waiting for the right time. Do it now and put it to one side. You can always come back to it and add more or replace bits. If you wait until you feel ready, you might be waiting your whole life.

Box Breathing

1. When you feel like you have low energy in the afternoon, take a moment to breathe. You may find it re-energises you.

2. Take back your power in any situation.

3. When you're struggling at work to think clearly, take 5 minutes out to bring in fresh oxygen to your brain. Exhale all the stale air that has pooled in your lungs.

4. Turn off the negative chatter going on in your mind to take stock.

Who am I?

1. Surround yourself with others that love and support you. Feel their love and respect and enjoy this feeling.

2. Show others your gratitude for being there for you. Make them feel good just like they have for you. What you put out to the world, you also attract.

3. Allow others to see you as you see yourself. This will give them permission to help you more.

4. Remember, the negatives are just really chances at improving yourself to become a more rounded person. They're not really negatives at all.

Order to the Universe

1.   Go into your heart to find what you really need and want.

2.   Send out your order when no one else is around. Wait for others to go to bed or take the dog a walk so that you can really concentrate all of your emotions on your order.

3.   Be open to all gifts and have faith that anything is possible.

4.   Keep an eye on all your dreams by creating a dream board. Look at the pictures every morning and evening and deeply connect with them. Imagine how amazing your life will be once you have them. Now, feel all your thoughts and emotions; connect them with your order.

Total Freedom

1.   Realise when you're having a 'treat'. Do you actually enjoy it or are you having it because it's easy?

2.   Imagine how amazing you will feel when the habit no longer has any power over you.

3.   Take all the negativity out of your life for a week. See what positive changes occur. Try taking out social media or stop watching TV. Only do the things that you can control. Let things into your life that serve you well, rather than taking in negative feelings. Only take in the things that make you feel great.

4.   Find a healthier alternative to the old 'treat' that will positively help you but that still gives you pleasure.

These skills work on their own but also work great when used together. They will help you to move forward and make you emotionally stronger. Once you've had a victory, make sure you celebrate!

If you don't use it, you lose it. Remember a time when you had a skill and you didn't use it often. The next time you tried to use it, it just wasn't as easy or didn't feel right. I took a break from running for a few months then, when I went back to running, it felt like I had never run in my life. The same goes for these skills or any skill that you learn. I still do the 'Who am I?' exercise because, if I don't, slowly but surely the negatives start creeping back in and I catch myself saying something that won't do me any good and stops me from moving forward.

Treat yourself like you want others to treat you:

Be kind

Be respectful

Be honest

Be loving

Be approachable

What you think of, you'll get more of; what you give, you'll receive back.

What's next?

Wherever you are in your story, these skills will work. If I can get over my darkest of days then so can you. The more you go through these skills, the easier they'll become and they will help lead you to break free.

If you complete a skill but don't connect with it straight away, leave it alone and come back to it at a different time. Just like when you watch a movie for the first time, you don't always 'get it' but when you rewatch it, you come to understand it better. You even see bits that you missed the first time around.

Know that I am with you every step of the way. You can email me at –
lg.breakfree@gmail.com.

The skills and exercises in this book are to help you cope with daily mental struggles and to help you get through challenging times. Rather than having slump days that easily turn into weeks or years, I hope *Break Free* gives you that light in your darkness and lets you know you are never alone.

Once you've worked through this book, you'll find it gives you the strength to open up and share yourself with the ones you love. Over the years, I have come to realise that joining groups on social media that are for 'abuse survivors' or those with 'chronic illness' are not always what they seem to be. Yes, they give support and give you a community to speak freely in – and I've gained some very close friends from them – but they can also drag you down with negative chatter. It's great to able to share with others that have been or are going through hard times but be mindful that they can also drag you down. Some groups can actually end up making you feel worse than when you first started.

Remember like attracts like – if you surround yourself with negative or self-loathing people, you start to become one.

Before I felt calm and in control of the conversations in my head, I hated spending any time alone. But now, I love having time to myself, either to relax and read, or have a pamper day! Time spent alone can be really great for us, allowing us to be kind to ourselves. Time alone isn't about being isolated; it's about spending time in your own head and enjoying it. When others see how amazing you're doing, you'll inspire them to make positive changes too.

Once you've finished this book, make a list of people that are important to you and that you trust. Go through your list and tell each person what you love about them and how much they mean to you. Don't forget to tell them that you value them for being in your life. This will make you both feel good.

If someone has been horrible to you for no apparent reason, remember that they may have things going on in their own life that they haven't told you about. Tell them why they have upset you and tell them that you know how difficult life can be sometimes. Explain that you are always here for them if they ever need you. This will give you peace in your own mind and it may help someone else that's struggling too.

I believe we all want and deserve peace, self-love and happiness. Anything and everything is possible but it needs to start with action. Just reading this book won't change anything – you need to go through the exercises and skills to start creating your better life, both internally and externally. We always get a second chance. It's called "Tomorrow".

We can't change our past. But we can always change how we feel and how we see the world. Allow yourself to grow from the past. It doesn't mean the rest of your life can't be amazing. It all starts with you – trust me, I know.

Don't forget, I am always here. Come and say hi! I look forward to hearing from you.

In the meantime, I am sending you love and light.

Thank you!

Acknowledgements

I am grateful to both my sister and my brother-in-law for taking me in and allowing me to find my purpose in life. For always being there whenever I or Mum needed her. I am grateful to my niece and nephew too for taking me back into their lives and letting me know them.

Thank you to my close friends that have been my light when I couldn't see and encouraging me to keep going even when I wanted to quit. Thank you to all the people that have come and gone through my past, they have made me into the person I am today.

This has been a challenging time for us all. As I wrote this, the Covid-19 pandemic was happening and I thank you all for your constant love and light. I love you all and I am forever grateful that I have been blessed to know you.

From every part of me, thank you to the universe for showing me my purpose and to God for always having a plan. Even in the darkest times, as these were, when I learnt my greatest lessons.

Most of all, thank you to all of my readers for allowing me to serve others and give you the love and light that you all deserve!

Special Thanks to

My copy editor for making my words flow so my books help people that need to hear that they are incredible.

Nicholas Taylor
Editor | Proof-reader | Writer

Further Reading and Resources

Break Free from Loneliness & Anxiety By L Goodrick

Find mental health crisis support services through the NHS
www.nhs.uk

Biblical references from *MyBible*
www.mybible.com

Allan Schore, 'Dr. Allan Schore on the Physiological Impact of Dissociation' [including video], PsychAlive, https://www.psychalive.org/video-dr-allan-schore-physiological-impact-dissociation/, accessed 17/02/2021.

Andrew Huberman, 'How to Change Your Brain' [podcast], Rich Roll (20/07/2020) https://www.richroll.com/podcast/andrew-huberman-533/, accessed 17/02/2021.

Barbara Jennings, 'Cell Phones, Dopamine, and Development' [video], YouTube (uploaded 02/10/2013), https://www.youtube.com/watch?v=kGZvNbfrNag, accessed 17/02/2021.

Blaine Oelkers, 'Unlocking the Screen of Your Mind' [video], YouTube (uploaded 26/07/2017), https://www.youtube.com/watch?v=xsrkOSTyWCU, accessed 17/02/2021.

Brandon Zhang, 'How a Dopamine Detox Reset My Life', Brandon Zhang Blog (10/05/2019), https://www.brandonzhang.com/blog/dopamine-detox, accessed 17/02/2021.

Cameron Sepah, 'Dopamine Brain Fasting: More Than Just a Fad, It's Science' [video], YouTube (uploaded 19/01/2020), https://www.youtube.com/watch?v=m1hRz4LbNO0, accessed 17/02/2021.

Claudia Christian, 'How I Overcame Alcoholism' [video], YouTube (uploaded 31/05/2016), https://www.youtube.com/watch?v=6EghiY_s2ts, accessed 17/02/2021.

Corey Waller, 'Addiction Neuroscience 101' [video], YouTube (uploaded 04/04/2018), https://www.youtube.com/watch?v=bwZcPwlRRcc, accessed 17/02/2021.

Daniel Z. Lieberman and Michael E. Long, 'The Molecule of More' (2020)David Steindl-Rast, 'Want to be happy? Be grateful' [video], YouTube (uploaded 27/11/2013), https://www.youtube.com/watch?v=UtBsl3j0YRQ, accessed 17/02/2021.

Gina Nguyen, Mirette Mounir and Sarah Muir, 'Dissociative identity disorder: Abnormal psychology professor reviews the movie SPLIT (Part 1)' [including video], Learning Technologies Lab, McMaster University (31/03/2019), https://healthsci.mcmaster.ca/learningtechlab/news/2019/03/31/ dissociative-identity-disorder-abnormal-psychology-professor-reviews-the-movie-split-(part-1), accessed 17/02/2020.

Jane Ransom, 'Discover the Three Keys of Gratitude to Unlock Your Happiest Life' [video], YouTube (uploaded 15/11/2012), https://www.youtube.com/watch?v=ewi0qlqrshE, accessed 17/02/2021.

Janelle Sinclair, 'Low Dopamine Symptoms and Causes: What You Need to Know' [video], YouTube (uploaded 04/04/2019), https://www.youtube.com/watch?v=d-7oIxK1OVw, accessed 17/02/2021.

Johann Hari, 'Chasing the Scream: The First and Last Days of the War on Drugs' (2015).

John Campbell, 'Nervous System A and P 8, Consciousness' [video], YouTube (uploaded 18/05/2019), https://www.youtube.com/watch?v=Gx7C3qa5FwU, accessed 17/02/2021.

Abundance Baked Bakery - Free photo on Pixabay

John Patrick, Jordan Peterson, 'How to forgive my abusive family without excusing their evil?' [video], YouTube (uploaded 27/06/2018), https://www.youtube.com/watch?v=yiTyYixkof0, accessed 17/02/2021.

Judson Brewer, 'A simple way to break a bad habit' [video], TEDtalks (November 2015), https://www.ted.com/talks/judson_brewer_a_simple_way_to_b reak_a_bad_habit, accessed 17/02/2021.

Justin Chadwick (dir.), 'Mandela: Long Walk to Freedom' [DVD], released 03/01/2014.

Kathy L. Kain. and Stephen J Terrel, 'Nurturing Resilience' (2018).

Kelli Sullivan, 'Nervous System: Reticular Formation' [video], YouTube (uploaded 02/04/2018), https://www.youtube.com/watch?v=DXcUQVSprA, accessed 17/02/2021.

Lisa Nichols, 'How To Turn Your Fear Into Fuel' [video], YouTube (uploaded 24/11/2016), https://www.youtube.com/watch?v=v19rDdIh_kY, accessed 17/02/2021.

Mark Solms, 'Reticular Activating System (RAS) and consciousness' [video], YouTube (uploaded 03/05/2016), https://www.youtube.com/watch?v=lk6RhycVP9M, accessed 17/02/2021.

Matt James, 'Intention Setting & the Reticular Activating System' [video], YouTube (uploaded 25/01/019), https://www.youtube.com/watch?v=LCw4OzJmZUY, accessed 17/02/2021.

Neal Barnard, 'Food Addiction: Why We Can't Stop Eating' [podcast], Exam Room Podcast (20/02/2019), https://www.pcrm.org/news/exam-room-podcast/food-addiction-why-we-cant-stop-eating, accessed 17/02/2019.

Nick Vujicic, 'Attitude of Gratitude' [video], YouTube (uploaded 05/04/2015), https://www.youtube.com/watch?v=Lm9BG712jdY, accessed 17/02/2021.

Nora Volko, 'Why Do Our Brains Get Addicted?' [video], TEDMED (2014), https://www.tedmed.com/talks/show?id=309096, accessed 17/02/2021

Oprah Winfrey, 'What Oprah Knows About the Power of Gratitude' [video], Oprah's Lifeclass (aired 10/28/2011), https://www.oprah.com/oprahs-lifeclass/what-oprah-knows-about-the-power-of-gratitude-video, accessed 17/02/2021.

R.T. Kendall, 'Total Forgiveness: Achieving God's Greatest Challenge' (2003).

Steve Harvey, 'Trust In Your Prayers' [Video], YouTube (uploaded 22/12/2019), https://www.youtube.com/watch?v=atqfkEwH5o8, accessed 17/02/21.

Tabitha M. Powledge, 'Addiction and the brain: The dopamine pathway is helping researchers find their way through the addiction maze', *BioScience* Volume 49, Issue 7, July 1999, Pages 513–519, https://doi.org/10.2307/1313471, accessed 17/02/2021.

The Dalai Lama, Desmond Tutu, Douglas Abrams, 'The Book of Joy' (2016).

Printed in Great Britain
by Amazon